How the Project Management Office Can Use Artificial Intelligence to Improve the Bottom Line

How the Project Management Office Can Use Artificial Intelligence to Improve the Bottom Line

Paul Boudreau

© 2020 by Paul Boudreau
All rights reserved. This book or any portion thereof may not be reproduced, stored in a retrieval system, or transmitted in any form by any means, electronic, mechanical, photocopying, recording, or otherwise, without the written permission of the author.
ISBN: 9781656629029

Contents

Introduction ix

Chapter 1 The PMO 1
                 The Value of AI 2
                 Why the PMO? 4
                 An Overview of AI Components 6
                 The Importance of Data 10
                 Summary 14

Chapter 2 Improve the Bottom Line 15
                 AI and the Objectives of the PMO 16
                 Project Governance 18
                 Develop an Accurate Scope, Schedule, and Budget 19
                 Reduce Project Costs 21
                 Increase Customer Loyalty 24
                 Expand Project Capability 24
                 Summary 25

Chapter 3 The AI Toolkit 27
                 Predict Project Success 28
                 Scope Analysis and Managing Change 34
                 Project Issues 36
                 The Budget 38
                 Resources 39

	Managing Risks · 42
	Lean Project Management · 43
	A Virtual Assistant · 44
	Summary · 48
Chapter 4	**Acquiring AI Tools** · 49
	Build or Buy? · 51
	Generic or Custom? · 55
	A Strategy for Implementing AI Tools · 56
	Maintain and Support · 58
	The Risks of Implementation · 60
	Summary · 61
Chapter 5	**Understanding Model Complexity** · 63
	Understand the Data · 66
	Steps to Manage Data · 68
	Understand the Features · 70
	Interpret Machine Learning Results Properly · · · · · · · · · · · · · · · 75
	Machine Learning Limitations · 76
	What Is Machine Learning Good At? · 78
	Summary · 79
Chapter 6	**The Ultimate Machine Learning Algorithm** · · · · · · · · · · · · · · 81
	The Unified Algorithm · 82
	Creating the Single Solution · 87
	Using the Ultimate Algorithm · 89
	Summary · 91
Chapter 7	**The Self-Driving Project** · 93
	Preparing · 95
	Executing · 99
	Managing Communication · 103
	Summary · 109
Chapter 8	**How to Deceive AI Tools** · 111
	Manage Your Profile · 112
	Communication and Browsing · 114

	The PMO as Change Manager	116
	Summary	117
Chapter 9	Sell the Solution	119
	Drive the Change in Methodology	120
	Sell the Solution	122
	Implementation Strategy	124
	The Pitfalls	127
	Overcoming AI Resistance	128
	Summary	129
Chapter 10	Changing Roles	131
	A New Role for Project Managers	133
	Can the Project Manager Be Replaced?	138
	Collaborating with AI Tools	140
	A New Role for the Project Team	143
	A New Role for the PMO	149
	Collaborating with IT Resources	155
	Summary	157
Chapter 11	The Future of AI and the PMO	159
	Trends and Challenges	160
	Ethics and Privacy	163
	Summary	167

Conclusion	169
Acknowledgments	173
Abbreviations	175
Bibliography	177
About the Author	185

Introduction

In many large organizations and in project-based organizations, a project management office (PMO) exists as an organizational structure that attempts to manage, control, and report progress on multiple projects. The PMO is an entity created to provide efficiency in an inherently messy environment: project management. The real world is filled with uncertainty, and the role of the PMO is to provide structure and consistency of results. Well, that is the theory. The reality is that projects have a high failure rate and PMOs struggle to find any means possible to correct this. At the very least, they try to implement project standards and are frequently asked to prioritize projects that must be successful.

Rising above the complex demands is the true PMO capability—the PMO as the driver of change for the project methodology. People don't cause project failure, and project managers are not the reason why projects fail to meet the scope, schedule, and cost objectives. It is the project methodology that is inadequately designed to consistently achieve project success. The PMO is the ultimate organizational body that can drive change by introducing artificial intelligence (AI) technology to the project processes and using appropriate metrics to ensure adherence.

The content that follows is intended not only for members of a PMO but also for executives, managers, sponsors, clients, and anyone else who is involved in projects. AI is a game-changing technology and requires a strong champion to promote and implement it successfully. The first chapter in this book discusses the value of AI and how to incorporate it into a business case. This chapter also reviews how the PMO is not a simple structure and that it can have several objectives that are not apparently clear or even officially mandated, and yet the organization can benefit greatly from pursuing these goals. Chapter 2 discusses many of these objectives and some of the capability that AI tools will contribute to improve outcomes. This section also uncovers some aspects of lean project management where AI will be useful. Chapter 3 discusses specific AI tools that either exist or are under development and will be available soon. This content is timely because AI tools for project management are being deployed now, not three or four years in the future as some people expect. Project management is an area that is becoming a new marketplace for AI technology, as practitioners begin to imagine solutions and seek improvements on how projects, programs, and portfolios are managed.

Chapter 4 describes the creation of a strategy for finding and implementing AI tools in the organization and the critical role the PMO will play in this process. The PMO also must lead the acquisition of knowledge about this new technology as well as become trained in how to use AI tools properly. The process of deploying AI can be fairly simple, but understanding the outcome in mathematical terms is more challenging, as described in chapter 5. It is important to understand how each component in the process, such as the data, the hyperparameters, and the machine learning model, work together to produce a result. This outcome must be interpreted properly and then applied correctly in order to guide good project decisions.

Chapter 6 takes a higher-level perspective and describes some of the current research in AI tools and the difficulty of creating a single algorithm for all purposes—or, in the case of project management, for all decisions that are made. The analogy of a project as a self-driving car for managing projects is described in chapter 7. This is a useful exercise that helps explain how AI technology can work in an imaginary self-driving project and uncovers some of the problems and possibilities with AI technology. Sticking with the more advanced capabilities of AI, chapter 8 takes a brutally honest and personal look at how to avoid the invasive aspects of the technology. We are already inundated with online ads based on an AI-created model of our personal profile, and managing how this will impact our professional life will be more difficult as the technology creeps into the workplace.

Someone needs to step up and be the champion for updating current project processes with AI, and no one is in a better position than the PMO. Selling the change to the stakeholders is the topic of chapter 9. Chapter 10 reviews the potential changes to roles in the project environment, a topic that concerns many people. Chapter 11 takes a more realistic look at what the future holds for AI tools in project management. The PMO needs to manage these changes effectively as part of creating a new and more successful project methodology for the organization. Issues such as ethics and privacy will also be concerns that must be managed with both caution and determination. These are deliberate changes with the purpose of seeking out significant value from project processes.

The conclusion reviews why this is necessary and how a new project methodology is a distinct project advantage. There are no guarantees and many risks when deploying new technology; however, the results can be spectacular and deliver a new sense of success in the PMO and the organization. AI implementation is both a challenge and an opportunity, and the PMO must take on this challenge in order to bring value to the organization.

CHAPTER 1
The PMO

Project management is at a pivotal moment in history, and the PMO has a crucial role to play in changing how we manage projects.

From two simple concepts—the ability to predict and the ability to classify—AI technology is changing the world. For a specific discipline such as project management, the ability to creatively apply these two concepts will radically change the way that project work is managed and how decisions are made. For a PMO, the challenge will be selecting and implementing the best AI tools that are available for project management and the ones that provide the most value to the organization. The objective of this book is to help with that process by identifying the capabilities of AI technology and determining how to change the project methodology to achieve the greatest benefit. The benefits include delivering every project on time and within budget as well as improving the bottom line by completing those projects at a lower cost.

THE VALUE OF AI

How do two simple concepts create so much change and deliver so much value? Think of a project that is represented by an image. The image contains all the contents of the project, including the scope, budget, schedule, risks, quality requirements, communication, resources, and dependencies on other projects. An AI tool can assess this image and compare it to the image of other projects that have been successful or unsuccessful. Based on that information, the AI tool can then classify whether a new project belongs with the successful group or the unsuccessful group. This is valuable information to know before the project starts and as it is executed. Other AI tools can be used in a dynamic approach where, on an ongoing basis throughout the project, they are used to maintain the trajectory toward a successful project completion.

A PMO normally has more than one objective in providing oversight to projects. Obviously, the main goal is to ensure that all projects in the portfolio deliver the project scope, on time and on or under budget. While the project manager has a clear focus on delivering a successful project, the PMO can take on the responsibility to reduce the overall cost of implementing projects. This objective might be due to competitor pressure or simply to reduce the financial burden on the performing organization.

Another objective might be to increase customer or client satisfaction. This type of goal goes beyond project success and involves the ability to impress the customer and create a bond of customer loyalty. Expanding customer loyalty requires increased vigilance for communication and all interactions with the customer. The organization must display a high level of professionalism and competence in delivering projects. The PMO may also want to expand their project capability in order to acquire and deliver far more complex projects than the ones in the current portfolio. The ability to achieve small gains on these objectives is too meager a goal. Significant gains are more desirable and can only be achieved by embracing and utilizing AI technology.

Acquiring and implementing AI technology is not easy because it takes time to gain the knowledge needed to understand the tools and to find or create the data required for AI tools to perform well. A survey of European AI start-up companies discovered that 40 percent of those that claimed to be using AI technology did not actually have any.[1] PMOs need to ensure that they are acquiring tools that actually use machine learning or some form of AI technology. Because AI tools use historical data, the organization must provide access to all stored project documentation. Unfortunately, 70 to 90 percent of the data stored by organizations is unstructured data.[2] Unstructured data includes email, images, graphs, and project documents that need to be

---

1 Dan Kelnar, "The State of AI: Divergence 2019," MMC Ventures Report, 2019, http://www.mmcventures.com/wp-content/uploads/2019/02/The-State-of-AI-2019-Divergence.pdf.
2 Christie Schneider, "The Biggest Data Challenges That You Might Not Even Know You Have," IBM, May 25, 2016, https://www.ibm.com/blogs/watson/2016/05/biggest-data-challenges-might-not-even-know.

read and interpreted by a natural language processing (NLP) algorithm. *Structured data*, on the other hand, is the term used to categorize data that is in a standardized format and properly labeled. This means that the AI tools designed for project management will have greater difficulty accessing and using the stored data.

WHY THE PMO?

There is no single, accepted definition for a PMO, which is an indication of the complexity of this type of structure. The Project Management Institute (PMI) defines a PMO as a body that provides a centralized or coordinated management of projects in an organization.[3] Other responsibilities include setting standards for project management and defining best practices. The PMO also gathers and reports project status for projects in the portfolio. The group, which typically consists of experienced project managers, provides support to project managers and project teams in their efforts to complete projects successfully.

The benefits of a PMO include the following:

- Delivering reduced costs by executing projects efficiently

- Providing a complete and coordinated analysis of the project portfolio

- Understanding the complete picture of business risks

- Ensuring that project decisions and interrelated decisions are aligned with the organization's strategy

---

[3] Project Management Institute, *A Guide to the Project Management Body of Knowledge* (PMBOK Guide), 6th ed. (Newton Square, PA: Project Management Institute, 2017), 48.

According to the Project Management Body of Knowledge (PMBOK), there are three types of PMOs: directive, controlling, and supportive (see figure 1). Large project-based organizations normally have a PMO, while many organizations do not have one at all. An existing PMO falls into one of the three categories. A directive PMO is sometimes known as a professional services department and they provide the project manager for each project. This group maintains direct control of the costs and schedule. A controlling PMO requires adherence to policies and procedures that include, for example, mandatory use of common templates as well as producing specific project metrics for reporting and conforming to a governance structure. A supportive PMO has the least influence, although it stills exists to provide resources, such as training or best practices in managing projects.[4] All these types of PMOs can be responsible for developing and promoting the use of AI in project processes.

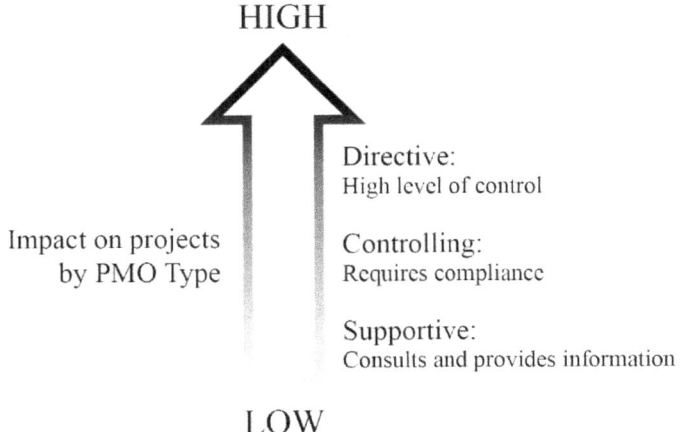

Figure 1: PMO Types

---

4 Ibid, 48.

The PMO may be responsible for either a program or a portfolio of projects. A program is a group of similar projects, such as information technology (IT) projects, while a portfolio contains groups of nonsimilar projects. For example, one program can be all IT projects and another program can be all human resources (HR) projects. The portfolio contains all project groupings across the organization. The PMO might only be responsible for one program grouping depending on the size of the program or the number of projects. However, it is still responsible for managing the interrelationships across the portfolio. For example, if an HR project is initiated to hire two hundred new employees, the IT project for expanding the network bandwidth might need to be completed first. Of course, many organizations are unaware of these distinctions or simply choose their own terms to describe a group of projects.

The most significant influence that a PMO has is to develop a roadmap for how to implement projects. This is known as the methodology that projects follow and is considered the standard or a control mechanism for the organization. If projects fail, then the methodology needs to be improved. As the project environment becomes more complex, the methodology must adapt. The PMO is in an ideal position to also develop a roadmap to implement AI tools and to verify the resulting benefits. It is a big challenge, and the PMO is probably the only group that can develop the plan for how to successfully implement these changes. In terms of adopting AI tools for project management, the PMO must identify the scope of work, including the boundaries of their authority, and to be successful, the first step is to understand the technology.

AN OVERVIEW OF AI COMPONENTS

The two main components of AI that will have the greatest impact on project management are machine learning and natural language processing. A machine learning algorithm uses a mathematical formula based in calculus that attempts to find the least error between correlations in the data. This is also known as minimizing the cost function. Based on the correlations, the AI tool creates a model that can be used to classify or make a prediction based on a new set of data. A machine learning tool is written in software code and often uses utilities, or pre-coded functional blocks of code, to create decision-making algorithms, the most popular and effective one being a neural network. Learning occurs in several ways, but the most common are as follows.

Supervised learning is when a dataset is labeled and the algorithm is trained to correlate each dataset with the labeled result. The algorithm is capable of modifying itself until it has the most accurate model. It is then used on test data to verify the accuracy of the model. For projects, we can also label our datasets. There are successful projects, well-designed risk plans, and communication plans that result in high stakeholder satisfaction. There are also negative results for each example. Supervised learning is commonly used in the field of health care to diagnose X-ray results and can provide higher accuracy than a trained technician.[5] The algorithm is trained on X-ray images labeled as either clear or showing evidence of a condition. A new X-ray image with a unique pattern is used as input to the algorithm and it diagnoses or predicts the result.

Unsupervised learning is when the data is not labeled but has a sufficient number of clues so that the algorithm is able to classify the data effectively. If the data indicates that an object has leaves, has a trunk,

---

5   Hanae Armitage, "AI Matched, Outperformed Radiologists in Screening X-Rays for Certain Diseases," Medical Xpress, November 21, 2018, https://medicalxpress.com/news/2018-11-ai-outperformed-radiologists-screening-x-rays.html.

and has branches, then the algorithm will correctly classify it as a tree. The main benefit of unsupervised learning is clustering. The algorithm has no labels and simply groups similar items together. How can this be applied to projects? Risks can be clustered or grouped so that when one of the risks from a cluster occurs, there is a strong possibility that a similar risk will occur.

Reinforcement learning is when the algorithm learns through trial and error to make proper predictions. A common example is typing on a smartphone, with the full word appearing after you've entered only two or three letters. The program learns your pattern through a series of repetitions in which you did not select the word it suggested because that was not the word you wanted. How can this apply to project management? All algorithms must be updated on a regular basis to stay accurate and this is one of the methods to do so.

There are several different methods used to create a machine learning algorithm, including a neural network, random forest, support vector machines (SVM), and a Naive Bayes classifier.[6] The algorithm creates a model based on historical data and then uses the model to make a classification or prediction based on a new set of data. Another basic capability of AI is NLP, which is a computer program's ability to interpret human language and classify communication into a meaning or, as it is called in NLP, an intent. This includes the ability to interpret emotion behind the words, which is a skill known as sentiment analysis. NLP is also used to search documents and extrapolate meaning and to determine correlations and anomalies. NLP-based algorithms can be integrated into project management tools. For example, NLP can be

---

6   Sunil Ray, "Commonly Used Machine Learning Algorithms (with Python and R Codes)," Analytics Vidhya, September 9, 2017, https://www.analyticsvidhya.com/blog/2017/09/common-machine-learning-algorithms.

used to search the text of a document and compare it to documents from similar projects. If the documents from similar projects are labeled as either accurate or incomplete, NLP results can be used by a machine learning algorithm to classify a current document based on the labels. NLP can also be used in scope documents or project proposals to search for errors or inconsistencies.

NLP is used to create models that allow a computer to interact with a human who is speaking. When humans talk or when they create written text, such as an instant message or an email, it is called an utterance. NLP uses utterances to determine a positive or negative sentiment with regard to a project environment. NLP can also be used to uncover utterances that reveal the threshold levels of stakeholders. In other words, the project status in terms of a late schedule, for example, can be above the tolerance level for the project customer or project sponsor who has the authority to ask for a complete justification and analysis before further funding is provided.

An intriguing benefit of a machine learning algorithm is that the same basic algorithm can be used with different data to achieve a new objective. Pedro Domingos uses an analogy to explain this in his book *The Master Algorithm*: "The human hand is simple—four fingers, and one opposable thumb—and yet it can make and use an infinite variety of tools."[7] Machine learning tools allow us to deliver increasingly larger and more complex projects and still achieve a successful result. There is a significant difference between regular programming code and machine learning algorithms. Normal programming code must ensure that all possibilities are taken into account in the code. Typically, if a particular event happens, then the code performs an action. Regular software programs are filled with logic that is required for every possible event; if something unforeseen happens, the code will stop. With

---

7 Pedro Domingos, *The Master Algorithm: How the Quest for the Ultimate Learning Machine Will Remake Our World* (New York: Basic Books, 2018), 41.

machine learning code, the program uses data to arrive at a probability and then uses that result to perform an action. If a new event occurs, the code uses the model based on data to make a decision and continues. There is logic in the code but far less is required than for non-AI-based programs.

The PMO needs to be the structure that provides consistency of use and validation of results for AI tools across all projects in the organization. The PMO can ensure that if a project manager finds a unique way to take advantage of a machine learning algorithm, it is shared with others. It is also possible that an AI tool does not provide usable results for one specific project or one specific function in a project and this must be investigated as part of a reinforcement learning process for machine learning models. A good reason for a PMO is the need to implement AI tools properly, train project managers on how to interpret and use the results, and constantly update the models with new data. Collaboration with an internal IT group, especially for data management, will be important, but the ultimate responsibility of the PMO will be to achieve higher project success rates and greater productivity across all projects.

THE IMPORTANCE OF DATA

The importance of data cannot be underestimated, and if data is managed properly, the machine learning results will provide enormous value to the organization as well as to each project. Data is objective and not judgmental. You need data to train an algorithm, and there are many problems concerning data when dealing with a machine learning tool. *Data wrangling* is a term that refers to the work of analyzing and preparing raw data into a format or structure that can be used by a machine learning tool. Because roughly 80 percent of the time spent in the process of creating a machine learning algorithm is committed to data, it is clearly an essential step.[8]

For most organizations, data is not clean. Data fields contain typos or improperly capitalized words. There is a variety of formats, the data fields do not have a clear meaning, and the contents do not follow a consistent format. Field formats are different across or sometimes within the same database. For example, a date field can be dd/mm/yy, mm/dd/yy, mm/week, yyyy/mm/dd, or any other possible permutation. There can be two data fields that actually mean the same thing and one data field that has two meanings.

During one of my projects, there was a data field for an owner's name, but it occasionally contained three names as there were three owners. And, of course, there is usually a column of data containing a single data field that is supposed to have a numeric value, and it is blank. AI cannot handle blank data fields. For project management data, it is likely that several files need to be combined or joined in some way so that the total data requirement is met. Another consideration for project data is the variety of file formats. The scope document is normally a text or pdf format, the quality metrics might be in a spreadsheet, and the schedule is in any number of formats, such as MS Project, Primavera, LiquidPlanner, or Asana. Therefore, NLP must be used to convert the words or phrases to usable data, which adds another layer of complexity.

Fortunately, there are software tools capable of scanning databases and finding unstructured data. There are also vendors that perform this task, although it is messy work and requires collaboration with the organization to clean the data. Data cleansing vendors that I work with

---

8 Gil Press, "Cleaning Big Data: Most Time-Consuming, Least Enjoyable Data Science Task, Survey Says," *Forbes*, March 23, 2016, https://www.forbes.com/sites/gilpress/2016/03/23/data-preparation-most-time-consuming-least-enjoyable-data-science-task-survey-says/#1ec00896f63.

are normally hired as part of a data migration effort, typically when upgrading to a new software solution. They are also available for software deployments, such as AI tools. It is easy to misjudge when the work to provide a structured dataset is complete. Organizations might retain a lot of historical project data, but the data needs to be processed to determine whether there any outliers that simply do not belong or if there are gaps where data is missing. The purpose is to take the raw data and transform it into data that can be used by a machine learning algorithm to develop patterns that form the model.

Data mining can be used in an organization to determine why projects fail and also at what point in the process or schedule they failed. The root cause can then be traced back to a document or process in the project that needs to be corrected. From this data, a machine learning model is built and used to evaluate both new projects and projects that are in the execution stage. Some of my clients ask about acquiring performance data from projects. What they mean is the ability to determine the accuracy of task estimates based on the amount of effort that was recorded to complete the tasks. When bidding on a new project contract, the analysis can result in more accurate financial submissions and, it is hoped, more wins. Some organizations are amazed by the ability to use vast amounts of historical project information and apply it to the next project. In fact, an organization that manages to collect the most information regarding a specific client will gain a considerable competitive advantage. This may already happen now, although in the future, the value of acquiring and using the data for AI tools will make this an insurmountable advantage.

In a project study from 2019, it was reported that for long-term, exploratory-type projects, the project managers often suffered from what the researchers termed *uncertainty blindness*. This refers to project managers who lose track of project history and are unsure of how to manage uncertainty as the project progresses.[9] Humans are fallible, and AI tools that have access to historical data can prevent these types of concerns in projects. The AI tools become subject matter experts in nearly every subject, assuming they have sufficient data. The project closing stage becomes more important for data retention and ensuring structured data formats. To support supervised learning, the project manager and PMO must think about adding labels to datasets throughout the project. A cumulative benefit can occur, which means that tools may start off less accurate, but as more data and labeled datasets are added, the tools will become exponentially more accurate and more effective.

Although projects are unique by definition, they have similar components. Consider a project to land a colony on another planet. This is certainly unique and challenging, so what historical data can be used to feed AI tools? While projects are unique, the more grandiose ones normally build on existing accomplishments. There have already been projects to land people on the moon, projects to send orbiters to other planets, and even projects on earth that attempt to simulate life on another planet. This means that we have some of the data and there is hope that the data from previous projects will still provide accurate machine learning results.

Companies such as Facebook and Google understand the value of data, and they use it to create personalized marketing profiles to provide relevant ads. For machine learning tools, the data may soon become more valuable than the software. A neural network can be coded in an open source language such as Python by using several lines

---

9 Leonardo Augusto de Vasconcelos Gomes, Vinicius Chagas Brasil, Rafael Augusto Seixas Reis de Paula, Ana Lúcia Figueiredo Facin, Frederico César de Vasconcelos Gomes, and Mario Sergio Salerno, "Proposing a Multilevel Approach for the Management of Uncertainties in Exploratory Projects," *PMI Journal* 50, no. 5 (2019): 554–70.

of code unlike the software developed for large, cumbersome, rules-based applications. It is the data that makes the neural network a productive tool that produces accurate predictions and classifications.

SUMMARY

Machine learning algorithms and natural language processing will change the way that projects are managed. Similar to other new technologies, organizations will struggle to implement these tools successfully. The value from AI is incredible, but it can only be achieved with a careful and deliberate strategy that includes both an improvement to the organization's bottom line and the ability to successfully implement the technology. The PMO is in an ideal position to make this happen. The PMO has the capacity to acquire and share knowledge, identify the proper use for AI tools in the project methodology, and manage the most important factor: the data. Given that the value of AI tools is undeniable, the next step is to ensure that they are aligned to the objectives of the PMO and, essentially, to the organization. This is the content for the next chapter.

CHAPTER 2
Improve the Bottom Line

Implementing AI technology has the advantage of moving the organization to a higher level in both project maturity and project productivity.

As stated in chapter 1, a PMO can have several objectives, even though they are outside the formal objectives defined for this group. To provide more value to the organization, every PMO must consider improving the bottom line, and there are two simple ways to make this happen. The first is to increase the top line, which is the revenue of the organization, and this assumes that the increase does not cause a disproportionate growth in costs. The second way to improve the bottom line is to reduce existing costs, which means finding a less expensive way to implement projects.

AI AND THE OBJECTIVES OF THE PMO

The existence of a PMO in the organization assumes that this is a project-based organization or that projects are significantly large or complex and justify the requirement for a PMO. A 2017 report from the PMI indicated that 71 percent of organizations had a PMO.[10] Although that seems high, I assume this means larger organizations or project-based organizations.

Typical PMO objectives include any number of the following:

1. Deliver the project scope on schedule and on or under budget for all projects.

2. Increase the project maturity level for the organization.

3. Ensure continuous improvement in project processes.

4. Reduce project costs.

---

10 Mary Ortega, "PMI 2017 Pulse of the Profession: Project Success Rates Climb, Fewer Dollars Wasted," Project Management Institute, February 8, 2017, https://www.pmi.org/about/press-media/press-releases/pmi-2017-pulse-of-the-profession.

5. Increase customer loyalty.

6. Expand project capability.

Within all these objectives, the PMO is expected to manage priorities. Similar to a project manager who has an overall perspective of the project, the PMO is expected to have an overall perspective of the portfolio and to make decisions based on understanding priorities that will optimize the benefit for an organization. All the objectives have the potential to improve the bottom line for an organization. Other functions of the PMO, such as assigning a project manager or training project managers, fit under existing objectives, particularly the first two objectives.

Another important role included in these first two objectives is to manage interdependencies between projects, which includes project governance. Managing interdependencies is a larger responsibility and includes both concurrent project interdependencies and managing longitudinal interdependencies. Concurrent interdependencies occur when two or more projects are being executed at the same time. Longitudinal interdependencies refer to the sequencing of projects at the portfolio level where decisions are made to start projects, terminate projects, and properly apply resources.[11]

A good analogy for managing a project is the self-driving car. There is a destination and a starting point. The vehicle needs to arrive on time and without additional costs. The car normally encounters events that have been dealt with before, such as a stop sign, speed limits, and a direction to turn. It is the unexpected events that are the most challenging to a self-driving car, and managing a project is similar. Most events are straightforward and the project team knows how to manage them.

---

11 Alexander Kock and Hans Georg Gemünden, "Project Lineage Management and Project Portfolio Success," *PMI Journal* 50, no. 5 (2019): 587–601.

Managing unusual or unexpected events poses the greatest challenge, and this is the area where AI tools provide the most value in trying to achieve project objectives. Similar to the self-driving car, a project must be properly planned at the outset and then well managed as the project progresses. The following sections discuss how AI tools can be used to achieve PMO objectives in general as a precursor to a more detailed review of specific AI tools.

PROJECT GOVERNANCE

Regardless of the type of PMO, there will be some form of governance, which means how multiple projects are managed as a group and the structure that projects are required to follow. When managing multiple projects, the PMO might be responsible for assigning the project managers and for managing common elements across projects, such as resources, risk, or communication. Managing the common aspects must be efficient and effective. In this case, efficiency refers to how quickly the work is performed and the amount of resources required. Effectiveness refers to the results of PMO decisions or project modifications that positively or negatively affect project outcomes. Both the efficiency and the effectiveness of PMO decisions can be improved with AI tools.

This governance structure includes a standard for how projects are approved and implemented and also defines the metrics for project success. Therefore, if the governance model is ineffective, it needs to change so that project success rates are higher and outcomes are more predictable. In a large organization, the PMO can be responsible for maintaining the project information repository, and this activity will be more valuable as AI tools are implemented.

The PMO can increase the project maturity of the organization in many ways, with the two main areas being training and awareness. Both of these will be required as the project processes change with the introduction of AI tools. Assessing the value of AI tools and creating an implementation plan will be a critical role for the PMO. This is not a one-time effort with an end date. AI tools are part of an ongoing commitment to continuous improvement in project processes that includes evaluating success and removing unsuccessful tools as part of providing structure to the way projects are managed. The governance framework has an impact on many aspects of a project. The following sections highlight how the PMO, as the owner of AI implementation for project management, can initiate changes that will result in a bottom-line benefit to the organization.

DEVELOP AN ACCURATE SCOPE, SCHEDULE, AND BUDGET

The scope statement for a project must be accurate and complete, something that AI tools can help ensure. The goal is to instill honesty in the scope statement, which results in reduced changes during the project as well as the creation of a more accurate budget and schedule. Discovering deficiencies in scope and the eventual added cost is a positive development, and yet some customers may be mesmerized by vendors with the lowest-cost bid. Have vendors ever bid low to win a project and then used change orders to bring the cost back to what it should have been originally? While AI tools provide a better scope statement, the PMO needs to sell the fact that accuracy is more effective at the start of the project. Research confirms that there is significant value in catching errors early for software development projects.[12] Most project managers know that this is true for all projects.

This highlights a concern that is a frequent problem for project management: integrity. In an effort to please a customer, approval

---

12   Capers Jones and Olivier Bonsignour, *The Economics of Software Quality* (Boston: Addison-Wesley Professional, 2011).

may be given for what is known to be an incomplete scope statement. This results in an aggressive schedule and an accompanying optimistic budget in order to be selected to perform the project. The overseeing entity that must address this is the PMO. Starting a project with inaccurate or incomplete documents and a poor execution strategy will drive a low project success rate with unavoidable increased cost. Customers need integrity in project management, and achieving project success will build confidence in the process and in the credibility of the organization.

For managing the customer, tools are available that make this much more efficient, albeit possibly more frightening. Organizations such as Facebook and Amazon collect significant amounts of data on people, and it has been said that they know us better than we know ourselves. They know what we purchase, what we search for, who our friends are, and how we react to certain events. Facial recognition software is used at airports to match our face to our passport photo, and similar software is used elsewhere to detect emotions displayed on a face, such as happiness, sadness, and disappointment. Organizations capture the information for vast numbers of people and use it to build a personal profile of individuals. These profiles are used to identify the most effective method of interacting with each person. This capability will soon be available for managing projects, and the challenge is to use it properly to increase customer satisfaction and to build a bond of trust. There are tools available that capture personal sentiment, likes, dislikes, behavior patterns, and many other characteristics. The PMO can become the bridge that delivers specific information to the project manager about how to properly interact with the customer or project sponsor in order to start the project with accurate documents, commit to an achievable strategy, and deliver the project objectives.

REDUCE PROJECT COSTS

There are many costs in the project budget, and it is normally resources that incur the greatest expense. There are AI tools that assess the resource efficiency per task and suggest alternate resources to maintain the project schedule. Similar tools can be used to minimize the resource costs. It starts with the project schedule and assigning resources. There is an option to use internal resources or external contracted resources. The trade-off is made by determining the skills, ability, and efficiency of other resources, although sometimes it is strictly based on availability. An AI tool can help make the correct determination by analyzing historical data for the efficiency of task completion as well as by incorporating current resource cost data and variances based on skills. The objective is to optimize resources to achieve a lower cost for completing the activities.

As AI tools advance, there is an opportunity to reduce the amount of time required by a project manager to oversee each project, which is another cost-savings opportunity. A prediction tool based on machine learning algorithms helps keep the project on schedule and within the project's budget. A virtual assistant with an intelligent agent keeps the project team and stakeholders informed. The plan is to start the project with a clear and complete scope statement and a solid project schedule, with minimal changes required along the way. This not only increases the probability of project success but also reduces the constant oversight required by a project manager or the PMO. In a self-directed team approach, the project team members work on and complete tasks that are assigned according to the project schedule and highlighted by workflow reminders.

One of the most problematic concerns for a budget is risk. Each project has a list of risks that are assigned a probability and an impact, and normally the impact has a cost and schedule implication, especially if there is a financial penalty for missing a milestone. Therefore, both of these are budget concerns. With AI tools, the risks can be identified before the project begins and allow an opportunity to reduce the probability and the impact. This not only offers the chance to reduce project costs but also brings greater stability to the project budget. Imagine a budget contingency amount that can be kept as low as possible and still be accurate throughout the project. Another alternative that can be evaluated by an AI tool is whether it is more effective and less costly to outsource the risk to a vendor.

Delivering quality incurs a cost, but the benefit from a reduction in nonconformance is greater than the cost incurred. This is mainly directed at projects that create a product, although it has an internal perspective as well. Adherence to the new project methodology is essential to maintain the integrity of the AI-infused process. Deviation from the project processes can result in loss and increased waste, and both of these create a negative financial impact.

For the PMO, ineffective communication can incur a cost when it creates inefficiencies in resource assignments, resource usage, project interdependencies, and other similar aspects. Communication is especially important with a project sponsor, client, or customer, and ineffective communication might create a misunderstanding regarding project funding as well as a larger plan for future projects.

In many projects, budget constraints are initiated after the project has started. In this type of situation, the PMO works with project managers to reduce the project budget. Can AI tools discover the best way to complete a project by using fewer funds? If the project has a time constraint, then AI tools can be involved in schedule crashing, where the additional funds are used to complete the project ahead of schedule by calculating the most effective utilization of resources for the least cost possible. Alternately, fast tracking a project activity, where dependent tasks are started with some overlap in the finish-to-start relationship, can be considered, and AI tools can evaluate the risk of this strategy for both budget and schedule outcomes.

Similar to the way internet companies use data to create a profile, AI tools can be used to identify the best match for project resources that are assigned to tasks on a project. More importantly at a PMO level, the assignment of resources can be selected based on the overall optimization of all projects in a portfolio rather than on a single project. This provides improved results and reduces the time taken by the organization to investigate and manage the resource selection and assignment process.

The PMO can reduce waste with lean project management. The objective of lean project management is to provide the most value from completing the project while simultaneously reducing or eliminating waste. This can be a challenging task across several projects, although there is also the opportunity to coordinate activities to optimize the utilization of resources, for example. Projects can be very wasteful when delayed or poorly coordinated, and the PMO must consider all factors, including project interdependencies, to provide effective direction that can result in a lean process that emphasizes quality and continuous improvement to the processes. One of the greatest philosophies for efficient project management is a just-in-time approach, where work or materials are available when needed instead of sitting around in advance, which has a negative impact on cash flow. This is a double-edged sword, however, as the timing and coordination must be exact or the project will face delays. AI tools can support the exact timing and can assess risks as this process is used. In my project experience, project staff who are "between" projects are asked to go on additional training or to complete additional documentation. Idle project managers can also pose a financial burden on an organization unless they are redeployed fairly quickly to a project that has sufficient funding for the resource.

INCREASE CUSTOMER LOYALTY

The PMO is in the unique position of understanding the value that projects bring to the customer. It can also suggest that project goals be modified to align with a customer's strategic direction. If the project objective is to install software to reduce and contain costs for the organization, the true benefit might be to provide a platform that not only reduces costs but also allows for significant growth. Due to the speed and efficiency that the project results provide when compared to a competitor, this encourages new customers and new customer segments. In a fast-paced competitive landscape, strategic alignment to an organization's direction is critical in providing project value. The PMO can validate the business objectives and ensure that they are of strategic value and wrapped inside a good business case. Delivering the project scope on time and within budget brings increased credibility for the project processes and will enhance customer confidence in both the organization and the PMO.

EXPAND PROJECT CAPABILITY

To use AI tools for expanding project capability to new areas, one critical element will be access to data from similar projects. It may not be adequate to use existing project data when attempting to utilize AI tools on projects that are normally beyond an organization's capability. The strategy will be to acquire data from outside the organization and it is unlikely that competitors will provide the data, although it might be worthwhile to collaborate in some way. For taking incremental steps into new capability, an organization can evaluate how much data is available for the AI tools. Having developed a significant base of compiled data that is used to improve project decisions, the organization can proceed with projects that are outside their normal range of capability. For example, a construction company that specializes in small buildings can seek to tackle larger and more complex structures.

A software deployment contractor that performs configuration and installation for a single entity can expand to seek deployment opportunities across multiple branches or geographically diverse organizations.

Successful use of AI technology offers the ability to expand project capability in size and complexity and into totally unique areas. Of course, a business that completes projects for hardware development will not suddenly become capable of implementing global financial processes. However, as an organization grows or changes direction, the ability to successfully implement new projects is greater when using AI tools and especially when collecting larger volumes of project data. Some project decisions may in fact be more generic than specific, especially in areas such as risk, resources, or budget. A prerequisite to expanding project capability is consistently high success rates for existing projects, which is achievable by using AI tools in the project methodology.

The PMO can be involved with requests for proposals (RFPs) when an organization is bidding to win project work, and AI tools can improve the success of this process. Winning a bid can be a long, intensive, and time-consuming process with uncertainty of the outcome. NLP is used to scan documents and identify critical content as well as to make sure that all the requirements of an RFP are included in the response. Data mining is used based on previous successful bids to identify the critical factors that increase the probability of being the highest-scoring bidder. The process also saves time and cost by limiting the number of subject matter experts from various fields that are needed to review the content.

SUMMARY

The PMO has several objectives as part of providing value to the organization, and improving an organization's bottom line provides concrete evidence that the PMO is necessary. Implementing AI technology has the advantage of moving the organization to a higher level in both project maturity and project productivity. The PMO is central to the upcoming changes, especially if project managers in the organization are buried deep in managing existing projects. It is important to start projects with accurate and comprehensive planning documents and to properly manage projects as they are being executed. The PMO has the opportunity to find new ways to reduce costs, improve schedules, optimize resource utilization, increase customer loyalty, expand the organization's project capability, and implement lean processes. The PMO is the owner of project metrics, the key performance indicators (KPIs) of project success, and these are needed to benchmark the existing process against the changes when AI tools are implemented. There are numerous possibilities to improve the bottom line, and the PMO can build the business case to do this. The PMO can also focus on solving the pain that the current organization feels as projects go awry. The PMO is the clear leader in the change process to update the project methodology so that project success and bottom-line improvements become a consistent expectation and an enjoyable reality.

CHAPTER 3

The AI Toolkit

*The project methodology doesn't need Band-Aids;
it needs surgery.*

AI tools for project management are available now and numerous more tools are being developed. The challenge is to identify tools that are needed in your organization. This chapter is meant to stimulate thinking about AI concepts and to discover tools that can improve the project methodology. Some tools will be disruptive and change the way projects are managed, and some will provide significant efficiency improvements. Your goal is to select and implement tools that improve the organization's bottom line. AI tools can be used before the project starts, during project execution, or both. How will these tools fit into your organization?

PREDICT PROJECT SUCCESS

A project success predictor tool calculates the probability of success for a project before it begins based on a review of the project management documents created for project implementation. Typically, an AI predictor tool is a software program consisting of an algorithm that correlates patterns in the data using a supervised learning model. The data is provided from a series of historical projects that are labeled "success" or "failure" as defined by the organization. Based on the data, the algorithm calculates a probability of success for a new project. Why would an organization agree to implement a project that has a low probability of success? The capability of an AI-based prediction algorithm can be a powerful tool for the PMO.

How much data is required for a predictor tool to make accurate predictions? The answer can be determined by research and testing and may be variable based on the type of organization or the type of project. This is a problem that data scientists continue to work on. In the business world, the requirement is expected to be less than other fields, and for project management, this is an area that requires a lot more testing. There is likely a range of datasets that are adequate, and we are currently unsure about those amounts. Some organizations consistently maintain a project database for current and historical projects that is extensive enough to use as input for a machine learning tool, while other organizations do not understand the value of project data as it relates to the process for implementing projects. This is something that needs to change. All organizational data is valuable, and increasing project success rates will depend on capturing more data that can help improve the project methodology.

An ideal use for a predictor tool is in the project screening and project selection process. Project screening normally consists of a set of criteria that are used to screen out unsuitable projects. For example, the financial benefit may be too low or the time period for implementation might be too long. The screening factors can be both unique to an organization or common across most projects. The probability of success for a project can be used as an additional screening factor for projects.

Looking at this from a different perspective, the screening process provides threshold values for projects to receive further consideration in the process. The good part about using a predictor tool at this stage is that all projects are evaluated to the same standard. If one project receives a 72 percent probability of success and the second project receives a 95 percent probability of success, then one project has a clear advantage. The organization will determine what probability is the hurdle to achieve for the projects that will move forward for further consideration.

The project selection process aims to choose the best project from several alternatives. There can be many factors to consider, including the financial and strategic value of each project. However, the addition of a metric such as the probability of success adds a layer of confidence to achieving the objectives that are supported by the strategic and financial benefits. The probability of success can be included in a weighted scoring model in order to select the best project, as illustrated in table 1. This factor can also be considered as a stand-alone item that is subject to more scrutiny, as shown in the next section.

Table 1: Example of Project Selection Criteria

Criteria	Value	Weight	Score
Financial	Return on investment (ROI)		
Alignment to objectives	Rated factor		
Technical capacity	Yes/no		
Probability of success	Percentage		

Of course, you are likely to select a project that has a success probability of 95 percent instead of a project that has a probability of success of 65 percent. However, what if you absolutely must implement the project that has a 65 percent probability? It may be for legal, regulatory, or strategic reasons that this project is required. What is the next step when faced with this result? Logically, the project manager would gather the project team and rework the project planning documents. In reality, this means the strategy. As project managers, we are planners and we know that more work completed to create a successful plan will result in an easier implementation. Perhaps there is something missing in the documentation, or perhaps the strategy is all wrong. Whatever the issue, the planning for this project must be improved in order to achieve a higher probability of success before the project begins.

While a probability of success before the project begins may offer an improvement to project success rates, there are enhancements that will make this type of tool even more useful and possibly invaluable. Imagine a tool that can be used as the project is being executed to determine whether the probability of success is increasing or decreasing.

Pretend that the project manager is in a video game called *Managing a Project*. The project manager stands in a long hallway that has doors on both sides. The project manager walks along the hallway and then turns to the right, opens a door, and runs the predictor tool. It indicates that the probability of success for the project has now dropped to 45 percent. That door is closed, and the project manager walks farther down the hallway, turning to a door on the left. That door is opened and the predictor tool is run. It indicates that the project now has a 98 percent probability of success. What is happening? The project manager now has an AI tool that is helping and supporting the decision-making process in order to increase and maintain a high probability of success for the project to the very end.

This type of tool requires the identification and collection of specific project metrics as the project is being executed. This includes factors such as earned value management metrics as well as factors on which the project was approved, such as return on investment or payback period. In addition, there are environmental factors that can be collected, which include such external factors as the rate of inflation, the bank lending rate, or the duration it takes to acquire resources. The data collected may also include future metrics, such as the expected growth of the organization, the expected price of commodities, and the economic forecast data. AI requires a lot of data and can determine correlations that a human brain is unable to calculate.

Once the factors are determined, then an AI tool can classify a positive trend as helpful to the project, meaning an increased probability of success. If the trend is negative, then the factors are detrimental to the project, meaning a decreased probability of success. In addition, specific project decisions can be classified as part of a successful result or as part of a negative result. There are many other ways to use a predictor tool. That's the advantage of understanding and adopting an AI tool. It can be flexible to meet additional needs wherever it is installed in the project processes. AI can decipher data in a way that a person cannot, and it is an advantage to use this technology to complete more projects successfully.

Some organizations use a *gate* process to divide a project into distinct phases or stages. The gates are clearly defined milestones that are achieved when all the tasks required by that milestone are complete. A typical example is design-test-release. The gate also becomes a review and decision point in the project. This allows an organization to carefully review the project's progress and accomplishments. In addition, a gate normally has a checklist that must be completed in order to allow the project to proceed to the next stage. This is a control point for several aspects of the project, such as funding, quality, risk, and schedule. How does a predictor tool help? There are times when a project arrives at a gate, passes the checklist, and then fails miserably during the next stage. This is a cause for indescribable frustration. The predictor tool can help in a couple of ways. First, it might be possible that the checklist does not contain all the data elements that are necessary for the project to complete the next stage successfully. After all, it normally only consists of completed tasks. Has the risk increased since the start of the project, or what anomalies have occurred as the project progressed? The predictor tool can analyze historical project data and make a judgment as to the probability of passing the next gate. The second way a predictor tool can be used in this situation is to consider the factors that the project will face in the next stage and to correlate that data into a higher or lower probability of success if the project proceeds. This is also the point where modifications can be made to the project plan to increase the probability of success for the project.

The predictor tool of the future will be fully integrated with an organization's data. That includes historical projects, policies and procedures, strategic direction, and financial objectives. The predictor tool will not tell you what projects to implement to make the organization more successful, but it will tell you if the strategy and plan created for a project will be successful. The predictor tool will be seamless, interfacing with all the required data, whether that is internal to the organization on their database or external using the internet to capture environmental data.

Planning and execution documents will be read and interpreted using NLP, which will capture the values required for the machine learning algorithm. It is also possible for the tools to accept live streaming data from the project as it progresses. Above all, there must be a feedback loop that captures data and updates the model on a regular basis. One fascinating opportunity for the predictor tool is to include human factors, such as the personality of the project manager and project team. As AI tools develop more sophisticated methods to analyze and assess emotional status for individuals, this type of data can be included to improve the accuracy of project success probability and to identify potential project issues as early as possible.

Image classification tools are proliferating rapidly in many fields, especially in health care, where they are used to analyze X-rays and MRI results. Image classification can also be used in construction projects—for example, to determine the status of completion of a building or for land development. Similarly, an image or a snapshot of any project can potentially be used to determine the level of completion. This is a physical equivalent of the earned value management metric called schedule variance (SV). SV is a capture of tasks completed and incomplete based on what is planned to be finished at a point in time. This is a single metric that indicates project completeness but does not predict the end date of the project because that is based on the critical path. An image of project completeness helps determine the balance of project work that is completed early or is lagging behind and is a good indicator of schedule performance but does not include a status of the project's end date.

SCOPE ANALYSIS AND MANAGING CHANGE

The scope statement is a critical project document because it is a baseline that is used to create the project schedule and budget. A machine learning or NLP analysis tool can be used to verify that the scope is complete and accurate. A tool that already performs this for software projects that use agile methodology is ScopeMaster. A machine learning tool can be trained to understand the successful contents of a scope statement and classify content or identify missing pieces based on the data. The scope statement is a significant document that is used to create the schedule and budget; therefore, any inconsistences or errors have immediate consequences for project success.

An AI tool is ideal for managing change in a project. Based on the project scope for a similar project and comparing it thoroughly to the scope of a new project, an AI tool should be able to predict scope changes that will be requested as the project progresses. The goal is to minimize change during the project by ensuring that there is a comprehensive scope statement before the project begins. This also means that the other two baselines, the project schedule and the project budget, are more accurate. A machine learning tool is also able to classify how the change can be successfully implemented, and it can include a prediction of the impact on the project in terms of schedule and budget as well as the other knowledge areas. AI must be a holistic solution, and this is a good example where all aspects of the project are considered.

The process of ensuring an accurate scope statement requires an iterative AI approach. The data required starts with the scope statement for a project as well as all approved change orders. All projects and all change orders are used to create the model. Data analysis is performed to verify which change orders are identical, or at least similar, across projects. Each project is labeled as subsequently approving the change order or not. If the change order is not required, it is probably included in the original scope statement. The machine learning algorithm takes each change order one at a time and builds a supervised learning model based on the datasets. The scope statement for a new project is fed to the model, and it responds with a probability that the project will require the identified change based on an analysis of the language in the scope statement. This process is then repeated for every change order. It seems like a long and tedious process, but the advantage is that the machine learning algorithm that performs this is the same for each iteration. When completed, the project manager can be confident that the scope statement is accurate or, alternately, that the predicted change is added to the risk register and managed in a proactive way.

One of the great values of artificial intelligence technology is the ability to access vast amounts of data, perform analysis, evaluate alternatives, and make decisions. For project management, this is a significant opportunity. Consider the implications for a change request where a new requirement is proposed, and the project manager and project team consider the impact of the change on both the budget and the schedule. They collect data and respond with the potential increase in cost and delay in schedule. In reality, the change might affect numerous additional areas of the project or even other projects, which can create unexpected negative consequences. In a situation of several change requests at the same time, the complexity of dependencies may be too difficult for a human to analyze and develop an accurate evaluation. An AI tool can manage both complexity and vast amounts of data and can produce a more accurate assessment of the impact of the changes on the project.

Another opportunity is to use AI tools during the project when unanticipated changes arise. The AI tools are used to find the most efficient way to implement the change without generating a negative impact to the project budget and schedule. The tool can take a holistic perspective of the project and consider all other aspects—such as risk, quality, or training—that might need to be updated. This reduces budget pressures on a project and can ultimately decrease project costs.

Having properly formatted data should be easier with formal change request data because most organizations have good standards and common templates for integrated change control. There are two parts to this. The first is a change request log that captures all requested changes and whether they are approved, deferred, or rejected. The second is the actual change document itself, which typically provides an abundance of detailed data that can be used by machine learning tools. The lessons learned document from previous projects is also important because it may contain potential changes that previous projects did not anticipate. This can result in a machine learning tool that classifies lessons learned issues or predicts them as potential changes to the current project.

PROJECT ISSUES

As a project is being executed, there is normally a regular status meeting held either internally with the project team or externally with clients, or both. During this meeting or even outside of the meeting, issues or problems arise and are captured in a report known as the issues log. As project managers are aware, nothing ever goes perfectly on a project. Developing a machine learning tool to manage issues and problems consists of two opportunities. The first is to train a machine learning algorithm based on previous projects to predict issues for a newly proposed project. What is the likelihood of encountering a specific schedule delay, for example? At least by knowing this beforehand, the item can be added to the risk register and a mitigation plan can be created. The ultimate goal is to know all possible problems before the project begins. After all, project managers do not like surprises, especially negative ones and especially in the middle of project execution. The second opportunity for a machine learning tool is to recommend the best solution for any issue that occurs during the project. In spite of all the planning, there are unpredictable problems that will inevitably happen. A machine learning tool can use historical data to find the best solution given the nature of the project as well as how similar issues were resolved. Both of these solutions reduce project costs and improve the efficiency of the organization's resources.

Data, as always, is essential, and the input documents are critical because they need to include the lessons learned from previous projects as well as the issues log, with the outcome of the action taken to resolve the issue labeled as successful or not. The project documents are also key, as they define the project strategy and are used as input to train the model before the project begins. Having sufficient historical data will always be important. It is also imperative that the documents are formatted correctly and contain the proper categorization of the data. For example, in the issues log, the actions taken to resolve issues need to be saved and labeled as successful or not. In my experience, the lessons learned document can take many forms and is normally created with the objective of improving the project processes so that the issue is prevented from ever happening again. Once again, based on my experience, that does not always work. Most resolutions identified in a lessons learned document result in either procedure updates or ways to improve communication, and this outcome adds a layer of complexity to the training for a machine learning tool. The objective is to train the algorithm to recognize and predict similar problems in future projects, which can be performed by evaluating if the actions taken after a lesson learned have been implemented in the organization's policies and if they are effective. In addition, many projects do not document a formal lessons learned when the project has gone well, which increases the possibility of unbalanced data. Therefore, there is often no training data or very little training data available in this area for successful projects.

In an ideal project setting, a machine learning tool will be able to predict problems in advance and allow the project manager to take proactive measures to prevent them or resolve them quickly. In the event that an issue arises at the last moment, the machine learning tool can recommend an optimum solution based on what has worked in the past and considering the current project status, the organization, and the external environment. Both of these outcomes increase the probability of project success. Eventually this type of tool will be indispensable and can be connected to the project database for constant updates to the data and to further improve the tool's accuracy.

THE BUDGET

There are two main concerns that can be tracked with AI when managing a project budget: overspending and fraud. The project budget is different from an operating or functional department budget because it is a time-phased budget, which means that spending is variable for each time period. In an operating budget, expenditures tend to be the same or at least relatively consistent for each category for every time period. A time-phased budget not only has varying amounts per time period but also the categories of spending create additional complexity. For example, the project may need to spend money on materials as a one-time expense. Contracted services might be an ongoing monthly expense, although the amounts may vary. The variability of a time-phased project budget requires more sophisticated AI tools.

An AI tool can help to identify a pattern of overspending that will show a negative budget result at the end of the project. Of course, earned value management (EVM) metrics, such as variance at completion (VAC), will indicate the same result. The benefit of AI tools is to determine this pattern as soon as possible, which means that the AI tool will need to acquire real-time or near real-time data. Also, the AI tool can be more predictive by determining how the pattern of overspending can be corrected, an area where a project manager may have some difficulty or become defensive about project spending. A big challenge for the PMO is that project budgets are different—normally more complex—and that requires a solution that will still produce acceptable results. A tool such as BitWinder uses organizational data to analyze and predict results and identify potential budget and schedule overruns for large capital-intensive projects.

The second part of using AI tools for the project budget analysis is to identify any potential fraudulent transactions that are being charged to the project budget. An AI tool cannot detect fraud; it can only indicate the potential of fraud that requires further investigation and proof. Tools exist that perform auditing for an organization's financial status, such as MindBridge Ai Auditor. However, these are based on historical data, and, depending on how quickly a project progresses, it may not be timely.

An important responsibility of the PMO is to track contingency funds across all projects. The two types of contingency are the contingency reserve, which is held inside a project budget, and the management reserve, which is used at the discretion of the project sponsor or perhaps with strategic insight from the PMO. An AI tool can quickly analyze unused reserves from each project contingency after the tasks involved with risks have been completed, and this analysis of reserves can be conducted on a regular basis. For the management reserve, an AI tool can aid in decision-making by understanding the outcomes that each project offers and the probability of achieving the most important goals for the organization. An AI tool can also predict the probability or project success based on the new circumstances.

RESOURCES

In speaking to existing project managers and senior leaders, the tracking of resource utilization is a critical metric because it indicates the accuracy of the original estimates. Imagine capturing ongoing data from completed tasks and using that to update estimates for new projects or for project bids for other customers. This can be extremely valuable information at a PMO level. A machine learning tool can use the ongoing data to predict more accurately what amount of resource is required for each task, thereby helping to create a very credible response to a client in terms of budget and schedule for a proposal. This data becomes valuable for all future project estimates and can be updated on an ongoing basis to ensure that the organization is providing good quotes and making an achievable margin on the work. Conceivably, an organization that uses an AI tool that provides this type of accuracy for bidding on work has a considerable advantage over any other organization. This is one example of how data can be used effectively to bring value to an organization.

For managing multiple resources across project teams, a tool such as Epicflow can analyze the project work, assess constraints, and optimize resource allocation efficiency. A consideration must be made whenever discussing resources: task efficiency is only one part of a project, and as a project manager and member of the PMO, the entire project must be considered when making decisions based on AI tools. Moving a person from one task to another might seem to be an excellent decision, but it must consider any side effects, such as a degradation in quality or an increase in risk.

For the executing stage of a project, the project manager can evaluate the effectiveness of the project team. The health-care field is currently getting much better at analyzing and diagnosing individual health conditions, and AI is being used to determine health patterns in larger populations. These concepts are also applicable to a project team. The PMO can use AI to evaluate the condition of the various project teams or team members working on projects for the organization. Actions can be taken to provide additional support where necessary or to move people to different positions based on stress, for example.

If you are familiar with the Fitbit or Apple Watch, you understand that they are great tools for tracking a person's activity and hopefully result in a healthier lifestyle. People volunteer to wear them, and many companies buy them for their employees as a health benefit. Some people willingly share their progress with others. If an employer gave free health insurance coverage to anyone who agreed to share their data, a lot of people would probably agree to do so. There is also a facial recognition system, called Affectiva, that can determine a person's mood and state of mind. AI technology can be used not only to determine a person's habits but also to understand their emotions at any point in time. This can provide unprecedented power to an employer. It includes the ability to match the best person to a task as well as to track precisely how they are performing as the task progresses. This results in an optimization of resources across all projects and project tasks and determines the efficiency of each employee by taking steps to increase their personal efficiency in performing each task. It sounds invasive, but people frequently agree to their work conditions based on rewards, and if the rewards are sufficient, this type of strategy might not appear to be as invasive as it is. It allows an employer to track the progress of project activities in a similar way that a person's activity is tracked with a wearable device.

Tracking of stakeholders, including project team members, is becoming easier as new tools are introduced into the work environment. Companies are using new technology to reveal "psychology, emotion, social hierarchy, relationship quality, and much more."[13] Data science is now being combined with linguistics, psychology, and machine learning tools to evaluate and assess everything an employee says or does.

---

13 "Understand the People Who Matter to Your Business," Receptiviti.com, accessed January 9, 2020, https://www.receptiviti.com.

None of this is project specific, but the PMO has a role in determining how the technology can be implemented and used effectively for projects.

MANAGING RISKS

Similar to managing change, risks can be identified at the start of the project and verified if the project team has included them in the risk register. This is based on data from similar projects and can also include the risk probability and the impact on the project baselines. Risks also have the potential for creating a side effect or spillover onto other project activities when the risk occurs. A machine learning algorithm can understand this and predict the probability or ancillary effects on the project. As the project progresses, a risk may occur that was unforeseen. If this is an "unknown, unknown," as referred to in PMBOK, then it must be managed as part of the management reserve. However, if it is a specific project risk, the AI tool can determine the optimal way to manage the impact on other areas of the project. It should be evident from this analysis that the risk tool for machine learning can have several imbedded or multiple algorithms to help determine how to optimize the solution. The advantage of a machine learning tool is that, based on the data, it considers all aspects of the project and does not optimize a solution that creates a negative impact in another area. For a risk tool to be successful, there needs to be labeled data that is based on how previous risks were managed and the resulting outcome.

Risk management normally follows a series of structured processes or a set of steps, as shown in table 2. It also has a series of rules or practices that must be followed to identify, plan, and manage risks for a project. These practices are ideal activities that can be improved by using AI tools.

Table 2: Using AI for Project Risk

Example of Process Steps	Machine Learning and the NLP Process
Identify potential risks.	Review historical data from similar projects.
Assess probability and impact.	Use regression analysis to identify probability. Use classification to identify impact.
Categorize risks.	Classify risks.
Develop a risk mitigation plan.	Review historical data to develop an optimal plan using labeled data.
Receive an alert from the risk trigger (risk occurrence).	Integrate with the Internet of Things to identify risk occurrence.
Implement a risk action plan.	Communicate and implement a risk action plan.
Identify a contingency drawdown.	Recalculate the contingency amount.
Assess for residual risks.	Review historical data to identify the probability of residual risks.
Update the risk plan.	Generate automated updates to the risk plan.

LEAN PROJECT MANAGEMENT

AI tools are essential to support the concept of lean project management. While normally this is a reference to quality and the ability to reduce waste and eliminate unnecessary tasks, with the use of AI, it will accelerate beyond this capability for those who want to implement and use lean concepts. AI tools are about making the correct decisions in a timely manner, which is ideal for a project environment that desires less waste and more focus on achieving objectives. In addition, an AI tool can identify waste in previous projects and help a new project to avoid similar conditions.

Waste in a project process occurs as the project progresses but is normally only analyzed when the project is complete. An AI tool can identify wasteful or potentially wasteful practices from previous similar projects and allow the PMO to eliminate or at least reduce the waste. If this is not possible for an individual project, then it may be possible to address waste reduction and improved quality by implementing policies across a portfolio of projects. AI tools can be trained to support a lean project management approach and then used to reduce waste and minimize defects or rework in the process. The whole basis of using machine learning tools is to make the process more efficient. AI tools used in a project will reduce cost, optimize the schedule, and decrease the probability and impact of risks. These provide excellent value to an organization.

A VIRTUAL ASSISTANT

During project execution, a virtual assistant connected to an intelligent agent will become a vital tool to manage projects. For a PMO, this can also be used to instantly collect information across a portfolio of projects. Also known as chatbots or virtual personal assistants, these voice-enabled tools are frequently found in an instant messaging format on websites to interact with customers searching for information. The AI part is the ability to recognize and interpret sequences of words in a way that a response can be created. The request does not have to be exact because NLP can classify different expressions with the same intent. Imagine all your project management plans and current status updates loaded to a database and accessed by a voice-enabled assistant that can respond with project information instantly.

In addition, an intelligent agent is used to analyze the data and to provide project management logic and interpretation. You ask if a specific task that is due this week can be moved to the following week. The agent replies that this is possible because the task is not on the critical path, but it adds that a risk is attached to the task, and it will increase the risk probability from 20 percent to 30 percent. The agent identified that the task was not on the critical path and then identified that it was linked to a risk in the risk register. Finally, it gave the project manager an update on the risk characteristics. Now the project manager can investigate further or make a decision whether to move the task to the following week. This is a simple example of what is possible with AI tools that are currently being developed. It also illustrates the concept of ubiquitous project management, which means that a project can be managed from anywhere, at any time, as long as you have access to your assistant, and this is typically accessed by using a smartphone.

The data required to build a virtual assistant starts with all project planning documents and these are used to reply to queries about static information. During project execution, additional documents and updates are added to track the progress of the project. The most complex algorithm is one that provides the logic behind queries about project management concepts, such as understanding the critical path or how to reduce costs by prioritizing the scope requirements. A third level of documents may also include the policies and procedures of the organization so that any action can be verified as compliant with company policy.

A virtual assistant is available twenty-four hours a day, seven days a week, which is ideal for remote workers as well as for a globally dispersed team. Agents can provide an instant response and translate information into different languages. All this is great news as long as we learn how to properly work with them. Until the agent is fully trained and understands project management vocabulary, it will be important to phrase certain questions correctly in order to receive a response that accurately interprets results, such as project spending and the project schedule. It will be necessary to be precise, for example, by indicating a specific date or time frame for a project status. There may also be nuances of language that do not translate as easily, especially with project management jargon. The goal in using a virtual assistant is to improve communication, which provides beneficial results for managing projects.

The project can be managed from anywhere at any time, as long as you have access to your virtual assistant. It will also allow you to manage multiple projects at the same time. Simply invoke the project name for the latest updates. This is a great tool for a PMO, as long as the culture is one of openness and positive support. AI tools should be productive and promote confidence within the project team and project stakeholders. Achieving a high project success rate will solidify the tool as reliable and indispensable.

In figure 2, the process begins with an utterance, which is a request. A normal virtual assistant analyzes the request and classifies it as a specific intent or an objective. Next, it reviews the organizational documents to identify the information that can be used to create a reply. This is sufficient for simple information requests. An intelligent agent is included in the process to apply project management logic before a reply is created. For example, an intelligent agent can determine whether a task can be delayed because it is not on the critical path. An intelligent agent can also determine what tasks can be a target for cost reduction at the lowest risk to the project. The agent uses the same process that is followed by a typical project manager but is able to evaluate more data.

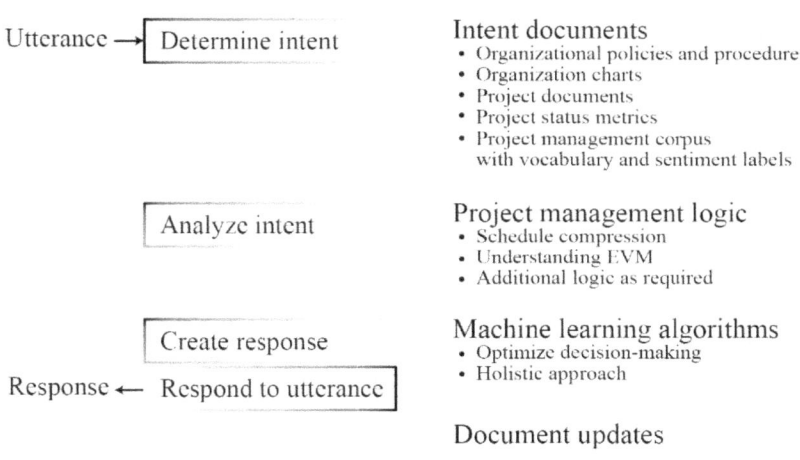

Figure 2: Virtual Assistant Process with an Intelligent Agent

For a project manager and members of the PMO, ubiquitous project management includes the ability to access project data easily and instantly and to make decisions based on input from a machine learning algorithm. For project stakeholders, it can mean accessing project information without searching documents or having to disrupt the project team. The project team can also access the documents and may provide input, updates, and opinions that are collected and communicated to the project manager in a summary format. In the future, an added feature for chatbots when accessed using a smartphone is to have facial recognition capability that identifies the person accessing the project information. In addition, the capability can be expanded by incorporating other AI tools, such as the predictor tool, expert systems, and simulation software, to turn this into a truly intelligent virtual assistant.

Effective communication is essential for the agile process methodology, and the PMO must evaluate and encourage new tools. Existing workflow tools, such as Slack, allow easy communication among team members and support several communication mechanisms from one application. Teamwork tools used for communication are a good source of data for learning more about the human factors for the project. However, machine learning is needed to uncover new details, such as sentiment, and the activities that are causing the most frustration.

SUMMARY

There are several AI tools for project management already in existence, and many more are being developed. It is important for the PMO to survey the landscape and to align the implementation strategy with resolving problems currently faced in completing projects successfully. The project environment will only become more complex, and the success rate of projects will decline unless there are changes. AI tools can assess the probability of success, analyze scope and predict changes, assist in creating and maintaining accurate budgets, improve resource utilization, and drastically improve communication. These capabilities can be used as projects begin and throughout the execution and completion of projects. AI tools need to disrupt the project methodology. They must take a holistic perspective of the project in order to avoid unanticipated negative consequences. A new concept of ubiquitous project management offers new capability if implemented and managed correctly. This is only a small sampling of how project management is changing, and it has the potential to add significant value to the organization. The next chapter provides insight into how the PMO can acquire the right tools.

CHAPTER 4

Acquiring AI Tools

*AI technology for project management will test our
ability to find and implement the right solutions.*

The PMO has a strategic responsibility to promote continuous improvement in both the project maturity of the organization and the success of projects. Implementing a new technology, such as AI, is critical to moving forward on these responsibilities. The PMO will be faced with many decisions, which include whether to buy tools or build them internally and also to determine the strategy for ongoing maintenance and support. Before any decision is made, it will be important for the PMO to take a step back and assess the amount of data that is available for AI tools. In fact, it is wise to perform some initial data analytics on the available data as a first step. This can be done with internal resources or with the aid of data analytics consultants. It might be possible to gain valuable insights into project issues based on data analysis alone. Regardless, a crucial first action is to check the data. There were at least two major software deployments that I worked on where the project was stalled due to data issues. I wish the organization had taken more time before the project started to investigate their data and fix most of the problems before jumping into the acquisition phase. AI technology for project management will test our ability to find and implement the right solutions and, more importantly, to perform this activity the right way.

Acquiring an AI tool to use in a project requires a good understanding of the data required, the process, and the desired output. The most common machine learning algorithms use supervised learning, which means that each dataset is labeled. Either the performing organization or the vendor needs to have the data that is required to feed the tool, and the amount of data and format of the data must be clear. Insufficient data leads to the creation of a poor model that results in a low accuracy of the output. The PMO also needs to know if there are hidden biases in the data and how to remedy or alter the data to mitigate this. A hidden bias might be due to historical data that does not contain enough recent projects or project data. Another issue is whether the labeled datasets are balanced. For example, if there are two labels and 98 percent are one type, the model will most likely predict that label for every new dataset. Can unsupervised learning be used for training a model? This is an area that is not as developed as supervised learning, so if this is being suggested by a vendor, there must be a clear understanding of how it works and what data is required over what duration of time.

An important factor to consider is the long-term strategy for developing AI tools as an ongoing process. If the organization starts with a smaller implementation, can the tools be scaled to a higher volume or larger purpose? This is the ability to begin with one section of the organization or a single project and then allow the tools to be used by the entire global organization. Alternately, the strategy might be a rollout of machine learning models from a single purpose in a project to all aspects of project management. Regardless, the solution needs to be scalable from a hardware, software, and data perspective.

BUILD OR BUY?

There are only two main options for acquiring AI tools: build your own or procure them from a vendor. The problem with buying from vendors is that, in the current landscape, each vendor only has a solution to a specific problem and that results in a disparate jigsaw puzzle of isolated pieces that may or may not eventually fit together. The tools could provide a way to improve the accuracy of project cost, maintain the end date for a schedule, or classify risks. These are all targeted in a specific area, and the problem is that there is no consideration for the overall perspective of the project. AI tools need to have a holistic perspective or integrated capability in the same way that we expect a project manager to take that responsibility. Having specific tools is not necessarily bad, but they can lead to blindly following outcomes that are not tied to the overall benefit of the project. In the case of the PMO, the piecemeal tools can have a negative impact on the overall portfolio of projects because they are so shortsighted. On the other hand, it is not wrong to use tools that have such a narrow focus as long as they do not detract or obscure the big picture of achieving project success and providing value to the organization.

Acquiring a tool from a vendor requires answers to specific questions. Will the organization be responsible for providing all the structured data, or will the vendor provide guidance or assistance? The level of support in this case is important, as the data will drive accuracy in the machine learning tools. Without proper data, the results will be useless. The organization needs to seek answers to the amount of data required to achieve accurate results, the level of balanced data that is acceptable, the expected hidden bias in the data, the learning approach being used, and how to manage it all. In addition, there might be a requirement to create interfaces to other systems in order to acquire and use more real-time data. A machine learning tool should not be created from a single acquisition of data and then ignored. Using ongoing data to provide continuous updates is more appropriate in a project management environment, especially with a fast-paced set of projects that are typical of the project management function. For the PMO, this means that data from several projects must be fed to the model, which creates the requirement to proactively manage data movement from the project or the project database in a common format for all projects.

In some cases, the organization can purchase an AI tool, such as the Predictor tool, from a vendor and manage the installation and usage within their internal capability. The vendor in this case provides instructions and guidance and then allows the organization to manage any level of support they require or want to perform themselves. AI tools have similar characteristics in that the organization normally provides the data, builds a model, and then produces results for their projects. Some organizations prefer to perform all the machine learning model creation themselves with the help of their IT department, although, once again, there needs to be a good understanding of the objectives before the model is created.

Some vendors are very reliable, so it can be tempting to utilize the skills of a familiar company and let them lead your AI tool deployment. However, AI technology is a different skill set and requires new knowledge. It will not be easy to distinguish between capable vendors and those who only want to sell tools, unless you know something about how the technology works. The first step is to get past any exaggerated claims because those are usually marketing puffery. The PMO needs to dig into the offering and verify that it is a good fit for the organization and provides bottom-line value. The most important consideration, of course, is the data. Assuming that the organization has data, the next question is: Who is responsible for upgrading it to a structured format that can be used by the AI tools? Even very capable vendors will be reluctant to perform this, especially if the organization wants a quick win without realizing the terrible condition of their data.

The second alternative is for an organization to create their own machine learning algorithms. For development of specific AI tools for the organization, there are cloud platforms that can be used to accelerate deployment. Most tools have subscriber-based pricing where payment is dependent on usage. As the organization develops and expands, the platforms easily adapt to increased usage. This assumes that the organization has some qualified internal skills to create models. Although the platform providers make it sound simple, there needs to be statistical analysis expertise as well as IT capability to understand the creation and use of machine learning code.

The scenario that requires the most internal resources is when the organization creates machine learning tools themselves using their own hardware and software resources. The benefit is having resources who understand the organization and are flexible in achieving specific goals. Another benefit is that the process can put more emphasis on the importance of data retention and data management, specifically for project management data. The PMO can then use this guidance to make sure that the proper data is collected and stored in a structured format for each project in the portfolio. The disadvantage is the requirement to maintain and constantly upgrade hardware and software platforms.

Acquiring AI tools should be based on a well-conceived strategy. The first step is to understand the existing situation with projects that are managed by the PMO. Problems that currently exist, such as the inability to achieve budget goals, are identified and then can be converted into objectives, such as "Ninety-five percent of projects started will be completed at no more than 5 percent over the project budget." Organizations need to clearly understand the existing situation and that includes the availability of structured data. As project managers, we know that a good plan is the basis for successfully executing a project, and acquiring AI tools is no different. Building a new machine learning algorithm might seem like great fun and a potential benefit, but if the data does not exist, then the tool will be ineffective. A comprehensive view of the existing situation must be documented. The next step is to create the objectives for the new process. As mentioned previously, the PMO must consider a change that disrupts the project methodology instead of simply automating existing tasks and roles. *Disruption* is a big, fancy word that means the project process needs to be performed differently, and integrating AI tools in the right way will accomplish this.

An internal assessment includes the capability to implement machine learning tools, which requires knowledge. The skills required include the ability to manage data as well as understanding how to implement and interpret machine learning results properly. Typical machine learning software can be written in a relatively small number of lines of code, so the difficult part is that the programmer must be able to translate the requirements into something meaningful. This is an area where the PMO can take a major role. The PMO needs to become trained in the concepts of AI, then be able to define the requirements in a way that can be easily implemented. The PMO can also participate in testing and then verify the results.

There are advantages and disadvantages to both building and buying AI tools. Building tools internally brings knowledge to the IT team and allows flexibility and more instant turnaround than the vendor process. However, there is likely to be problems finding skilled resources, especially data scientists and machine learning programmers. They command a high level of remuneration, and when they leave, they take a lot of organizational knowledge with them. Vendors can provide the expertise gained from numerous other deployments and make the process easier and faster. On the other hand, they also tend to have their own interests in mind and these are not always aligned with achieving organizational success. Finding a good vendor is critical because the organization becomes dependent on them as updates and changes occur. The PMO needs to evaluate which option is best, and that may be an ongoing evaluation

GENERIC OR CUSTOM?

An organization that is sensitive to cost may prefer a generic solution over an AI tool that is developed specifically for their environment and project type. A generic tool can be defined as an AI tool that is created to solve a project problem and can be used by different organizations because each organization has unique data. A custom tool is one that is developed based on a unique need or project environment. Perhaps it is a blend of the two options that works best for the organization. The PMO can play an important role in guiding the decision makers to the best solution. As always, the tools must provide a benefit in terms of increased project success and value to the organization.

Another consideration is a generic algorithm that is used by the organization for different purposes. For example, it is possible that the algorithm that creates a model for effectively managing change control can be reused with different data for training a model for resolving project issues. In fact, the reusability of algorithms can be a great cost savings. On the other hand, there needs to be an evaluation of how much one algorithm can successfully accomplish.

There are trade-offs between tweaking a model for one purpose and yet still using it for a slightly different purpose. This is an area where the PMO must navigate carefully, and it starts by being knowledgeable about AI tools in general, project problems, and the availability of data.

A STRATEGY FOR IMPLEMENTING AI TOOLS

Is the PMO ready to implement AI tools, and what approach will be taken? In his book *The AI Advantage: How to Put the Artificial Intelligence Revolution to Work*, Thomas Davenport argues that doing nothing is a dangerous choice.[14] Moving too quickly or too slowly is also problematic, but they are better alternatives. If the PMO is ready to implement AI tools, the organization needs to take positive steps in accepting AI and matching capabilities with problems to ensure that the outcomes are beneficial.

Numerous AI tools for project management are now available and more are on the way. How does the PMO know which tools are best suited to their project methodology and will provide the most value to the organization? AI is becoming a pervasive buzzword that can be used to blur the objective. Project organizations might be eager to implement AI tools, but it requires a sound strategy to be successful and achieve the value. Here are some recommended strategies:

---

14 Thomas H. Davenport, *The AI Advantage: How to Put the Artificial Intelligence Revolution to Work* (Cambridge, MA: MIT Press, 2018).

- Investigate what decisions need to be made in order for AI software and data to be added to the existing IT infrastructure.

- Determine where AI tools can provide the most benefit. What is the greatest pain: cost overrun, late due dates, resource availability, or other issues?

- Develop a good business case for changing the project methodology and promote the value of adding AI tools.

- Develop a set of clear policies and procedures for retention of project data and data standards.

- Publicize the value of project data and set standards for nomenclature and retention.

- Ensure proper project manager training so that they have adequate knowledge of managing data, interpreting results, and using AI tools correctly.

- Work with project managers to test the effectiveness of AI tools.

- Review and update the role of project managers and project team members in the organization.

- Document the changes to the project methodology and monitor to ensure adherence as this becomes the controllable standard for continuous improvement.

A strategy begins by understanding the current situation before determining what the end results should be. The PMO needs to evaluate the organization's readiness and desire to acquire AI tools. An assessment may be required to evaluate whether the capability to develop AI tools internally or externally is a better option. It might be a combination of both. A decision is also required for the use of internal or external resources to manage data issues. Because tools are dependent on data, there also must be a strategy for preparing the data or at least finding a data scientist to help with the datasets. You don't need a million pixels to recognize a face, and you don't need to see all the letters to know the word.[15] This is proof that data can be sampled and still represent the actual result. You rarely need an entire dataset for machine learning, and with large datasets, it is a good practice to perform some analysis to find the most representative data without damaging or reducing the significance. This process is called dimensionality reduction and is used to handle huge datasets.

Who is capable of performing these tasks? There are vendors and software tools that help clean data and add the proper label to each dataset.[16] You might be lucky and already have a good data scientist in the organization. As stated previously, good data scientists are difficult to find, and the saying goes that when data scientists discover a way to build an amazing machine learning model, they try to use it to make money in the stock market.

MAINTAIN AND SUPPORT

As previously mentioned, machine learning tools need ongoing updates, especially in terms of data to keep the models current and meaningful. New tools will be acquired and older tools can be retired, although decommissioning a tool will not be as frequent for typical

---

15   I base this on the game of hangman or its television version, *Wheel of Fortune*.
16   "Programmatically Building and Managing Training Data," Snorkel.org, accessed January 9, 2020, https://www.snorkel.org.

software that is based on a defined set of rules or logic. AI tools are more data driven, and the algorithm that is used to create a model is stable and less susceptible to technology or environmental changes.

The amount and frequency of support activities will depend largely on the strategic decisions made in acquiring the tools. One major concern will be the location of the data being used by the AI tools and whether the vendor or cloud provider stores a copy of the data. That has implications for privacy and security, which is discussed in a later chapter. Allowing vendors access to your data is dangerous because they can still retain privacy of the data but use it to build a model themselves that is used by a different organization.

There is a third option that is a blend of make or buy. With this selection, the decision is about how much of a vendor's services should be purchased and how much work will remain within the organization. There is a growing number of vendor-based IT resources and services available, as well as several cloud-based providers, that include machine learning capability as part of their services. It is best to gain knowledge about these solutions, preferably from someone who has experience with each one, because the descriptive language and marketing content tend to simplify yet overstate the actual capability. Here is only a small sampling of what is available:

AWS cloud. Amazon Web Services includes machine learning capability and pre-trained services, such as computer vision, language processing, and forecasting. This site provides developers with the ability to quickly build and deploy machine learning models with a workflow that includes data labels and data preparation as well as how to tune models to optimize them for deployment. That's mainly a marketing description because the work is more complex than it sounds.

Heroku. This is a cloud-based platform for building applications and is frequently used by start-ups for the free sandbox. It has the ability to scale with the business and supports numerous software languages. This is a primary selection for my researchers to host their software.

Google AutoML. Google offers a suite of tools to perform machine learning, which allows developers with limited expertise to build and train models. AutoML includes a labeling service as well as support for data cleansing, which results in high-quality data for the algorithms.

Twilio Autopilot. This website allows users to quickly build chatbots that function for a variety of online and mobile apps. Once again, it sounds good, but the reality is more complex when attempting to build applications for project management.

THE RISKS OF IMPLEMENTATION

Acquiring and implementing AI tools is a great opportunity, and similar to all changes, there are risks. The first risk is security and privacy. Will the people who have access to the model results also have access to the training data? In some cases, this is a good thing. On the other hand, for sensitive data, restrictions need to be considered and any loopholes must be closed. There is also the possibility of data infiltration. Think of this as a malicious virus intended to corrupt a system or something like ransomware where the owner of an infected system is asked to pay a fee to unlock databases. An attack on training data can result in disastrous consequences, mainly with a decision to perform the exact opposite of what a true machine learning algorithm would normally produce with good data. I don't know why some people are malicious, but it happens. Let's say a country is in the process of launching an extremely valuable satellite into space. A dissident group hacks into the launch system database and adds fake data to the machine learning training datasets. The launch fails and the dissidents expose their work so that they can take credit and gain publicity. Organizations need to secure the data against data attacks similar to the efforts that are already underway currently for many organizations. The difference is that attacks on machine learning datasets are likely to be less noticeable but they produce bad results.

A second risk is biased data, something already mentioned elsewhere. There needs to be a commonsense assessment of machine learning results in order to validate the outcome. There are times when a machine learning result is accurate based on the data but the data itself is not representative of the current environment. Another risk is poor extrapolation of data or incorrectly interpreting statistics. It has been suggested that a budget allocation be set aside for auditing or validating machine learning results.[17] These issues will be downplayed by vendors, and in the early days of AI, the occurrences of these types of risk are low. That will change as AI becomes more pervasive, and the biggest risk is that you have a problem in the AI tools that goes completely unnoticed. There are always risks with new technology, and the most reasonable response is to become knowledgeable in how to manage or eliminate the risks the same way that we reduce or eliminate the probability and impact in project risks.

SUMMARY

The process for acquiring AI tools has some common steps as well as some unique challenges when dealing with software. A common aspect is the decision whether to purchase tools or attempt to build them internally, which is more commonly referred to as the decision to make or buy. There are advantages and disadvantages to each choice, and the PMO can determine the evaluation criteria and guide the

---

17   Daniel Shapiro and Khalid El Emam, "Managing the Risks from AI Algorithms," Replica Analytics, December 10, 2019, https://replica-analytics.com/blog/blog/risks-from-AI-algorithms.

decision-making process. The ability to reuse machine learning models requires an assessment of where and how these tools will be used. Reusing models can be financially appealing, but this strategy must be carefully planned or it could become a serious pitfall. If the decision is made to acquire tools from a vendor, the PMO needs to determine the next process steps. As for all IT software, an ongoing support strategy is also required. Selecting a vendor includes giving the vendor access to the organization's data. The evaluation goes beyond simply acquiring an AI tool and includes creating a partnership that continues for considerable time and could be difficult to break. These are all serious concerns for a PMO that is simply looking to acquire new technology, and, although good decisions are required, the process must be efficient and timely.

CHAPTER 5
Understanding Model Complexity

The PMO must understand the limitations of AI as well as the opportunities.

As shown in figure 3, a typical machine learning model does not look complicated. Data is provided for validation and preprocessing, then the results are delivered to the machine learning algorithm, which performs training and testing to create a model. The outcome of the model is new knowledge that the human brain could not possibly derive. The model itself is fairly straightforward to create and does not take a significant number of lines of code, which leads to the inevitable conclusion that the data is an extremely important part of the process. Indeed, this flips current software wisdom on its head, as the data is now potentially more valuable than the software.

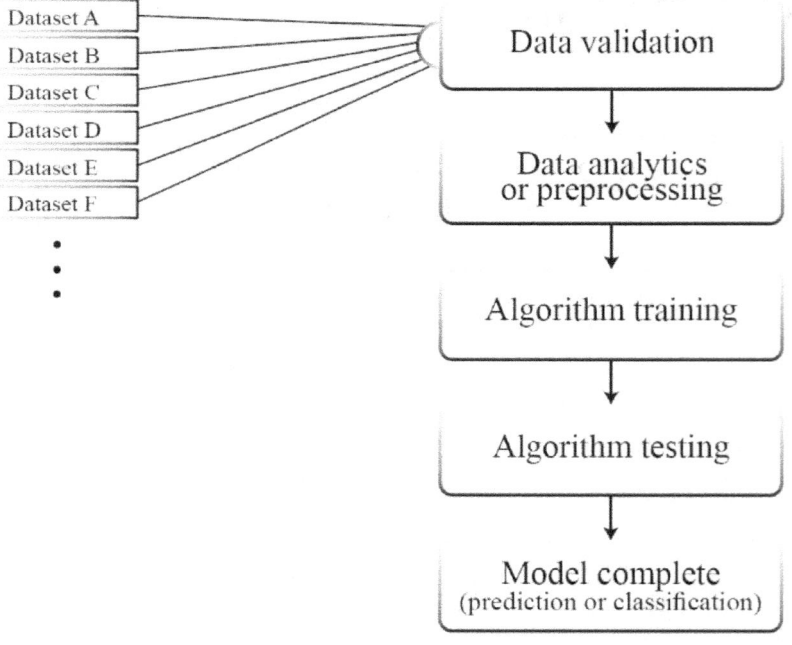

Figure 3. A Typical Machine Learning Model Structure

The knowledge gained from the data is very powerful, and the following is an example. It is a mystery in the medical field why, for example, some people who smoke do not contract lung cancer and some nonsmokers do get lung cancer. There is a correlation between smoking and lung cancer, but there are exceptions. I always thought that for any kind of cancer, there is a long equation that can determine exactly if a person is going to contract lung cancer, or any cancer for that matter. The equation probably contains hundreds, or even thousands, of variables, such as diet, genetics, living circumstances, income, and perhaps even birth order. Who knows? However, with a machine learning algorithm, all the data can be used to create a model and then the model can make a truly accurate prediction. Of course, it depends on having all the data, but the purpose of this example is to show that the person who owns the equation would have an extremely valuable asset. What if a model could determine the expected medical reason for how you are going to die as well as your life span to within a few months?

Now let's shift this to project management and to a machine learning algorithm that is developed to correlate the data in a model that identifies how projects in a specific industry can be successful. The model considers everything: the scope statement, risks, resources, material, task dependencies, quality, communication, and more. The value of that knowledge is a huge competitive advantage for private organizations and a large gain in productivity for any organization. Constructing a comprehensive model that considers all aspects of a project is not easy. However, the basic components are the same for any model in that a sufficient amount of structured data is required and the model needs to be trained and interpreted properly. Because data is so critical to the model, it is important to quickly resolve any issues regarding data, as data is used as a starting point for being able to understand and interpret the results.

UNDERSTAND THE DATA

A machine learning tool uses the data to make correlations and then calculates a prediction based on regression analysis. For a new set of data, it tries to find how close the new dataset matches the labeled datasets. In other words, how closely does the new dataset match the dataset labeled as a project success? From the sample data, the machine learning tool creates a model of what a successful project contains in terms of data. With a new dataset, the model then creates a prediction of how closely the correlation matches the labeled data. The resulting probability of success is then expressed as a percentage. The results of machine learning can be similar to a political poll that says the results are accurate to within 5 percentage points nine times out of ten. A machine learning output can be 100 percent representative of the data but only accurate 80 percent of the time.

How reliable is the result? If the datasets are all using the same model, then the relative comparison is easy. The regression percentage will be a good relative ranking of the project results. However, there are two basic problems when generating models. The first is underfitting, when there is not enough data to create an accurate model, so the results will be unreliable. The second problem is overfitting, when a model tries to include outliers, which distorts the limits of model accuracy.

One of the problems with data is that a model may produce a correlation but the correlation may not be causal. One of my frequently used examples is that the crime rate is higher where there are more churches. In fact, there is a direct correlation between the number of churches and the crime rate in a city. Is it a causal correlation? Do churches cause an increase in crime? No. The truth is that the number of churches in a city is normally based on the population and it is population density that is the reason for higher crime rates. This is an example of how misleading a simple correlation can be, and it is important to remember this when interpreting the results of machine learning.

To identify a causal correlation, take the time to look at the data and find out how it relates to the label. Perhaps features simply relate to each other, which means that the dataset can be reduced. That serves two functions: less data to manage and a more accurate model because the subdependent data is not included. Before the model is created, it is wise to sample the data to look for hidden bias. This occurs because the data is historical and becomes less relevant as time passes. You don't want to include sample data about cars from the 1920s because it would be skewed by the number of horse-drawn carriages still in the streets. Determining how much historical data should be used is a decision that must be carefully considered. There are times when the results need to be validated by using your own logic to ensure that the model has produced a sensible outcome. If true, this means that the data is a good representation of the labels and can be used to create a reliable machine learning model.

I worked on a project that was migrating data to a new system. The old system was more than thirty years old and the data needed to be cleaned and validated. There was one data field that captured a name, and the system provided self-service for owners to enter their names. The new system required a single name to be linked to the payment system, and yet some data fields in this set contained three different names. When asked, the owner simply replied, "It was purchased for the whole family, so I put all our names in." This story highlights that bad data is easily captured, even if it is not the intention. This relates to the validation of machine learning results, where looking at the data may explain a result that appears to be inaccurate. It also indicates that data analysis is often required before building the machine learning model.

STEPS TO MANAGE DATA

Here are several steps to take to create structured data. They look sequential, although the best approach is to think of them as cyclical or as an iterative process.[18]

1. *Identify the data required.* This is about aligning the data to the objective of the algorithm. If the objective is to learn about project interdependencies, then make sure that the data reflects this and not a single independent project.

2. *Structure the data.* This step requires that the data is readable, formatted properly, has a consistent format within fields, and is easily accessible. It includes the creation of labels where possible and might require NLP to identify data contained inside documents that are not in a database format.

3. *Clean the data.* The data needs to have errors removed. Blank data fields that are supposed to contain a numeric value are unacceptable, so a decision is required on how to fill them. Outliers also must be identified and resolved or categorized.

4. *Enrich the data if necessary.* Is there more data that can help with the results? If there is a gap in the data, an action can be taken to review and possibly find the missing data. Also, perhaps creating a field with derived data would help—that is, taking several data fields and performing a calculation, such as average or range.

---

18 "What Is Data Wrangling?," Trifacta.com, accessed January 9, 2020, https://www.trifacta.com/data-wrangling.

5. *Validate the usefulness of the data.* This step is confirming the accuracy of the data. For machine learning, it means assessing if the dataset has a reasonable balance of labeled datasets and is sufficiently diverse to be used for training.

6. *Make the data available and document the analysis.* This activity ensures that datasets are available and that the steps taken to prepare the data are documented so that any manipulations are identified. This document can be used to better understand or interpret the results.

Building a model using a neural network might be the "cool" thing to do, but a neural network is not the only machine learning method. To create a robust and reliable model, the programmer can try other algorithms, such as SVM or random forest, and evaluate the differences. A simple solution may often be the best one, and different models may have an impact on other factors, such as time to run the program or the ability to manage a higher volume of data. The objective is to create an algorithm that is useful in solving problems.

Hyperparameters are values that are determined before the machine learning algorithm begins the training process and can have an impact on the speed of the algorithm as well as on the quality of the results. Typically, they include the number of iterations specified for the learning process and, in a neural network, the number of layers that will be used in the training process. Tuning the hyperparameters refers to the opportunity to modify these values that control the creation of the model. However, experiential results from model builders suggest that changes to hyperparameters have only a small impact on the accuracy of the model.[19] Having a good dataset and creating the model based on the objective are the main factors for success.

There is often a problem with unbalanced data. Unbalanced data means that the dataset labels are not evenly distributed, which causes a problem with the accuracy of the results. For example, if the labels for every historical risk indicate that they will all result in a massive budget problem, then every new risk will be classified the same. A balanced dataset means that some risks are classified as a problem and others are not. With a balanced dataset, a new risk can be more easily correlated. Can unbalanced datasets be useful? Yes, as long as the limitations are understood. Machine learning results can be less than perfect but they can be still be useful for solving problems when the alternative is no results at all. In these situations, the algorithm might not achieve the original goal. However, it might be very useful for understanding specific situations.

UNDERSTAND THE FEATURES

Table 3 represents the data format for the input to the predictor tool using supervised learning, but this can be used for many other machine learning algorithms, including several that I mention in chapter 3. Each row contains data for one specific project, and each column contains a value of 1 or 0, which represents whether the defined feature is present or not. A *feature* is machine learning terminology and should be thought of as a characteristic of the project or as specific content that can be found in the project documents. For example, in the predictor tool, some of the features defined include a requirements traceability matrix, a risk owner, and a standardized change management process. These features do not necessarily result in a better project.

---

19   Steve Rochefort, "Practical Challenges in ML Workflows" (lecture, Machine Learning and Artificial Intelligence Ottawa, Ontario, CA, September 9, 2019).

The objective is to take many features from many project datasets and determine a correlation. Every organization might be unique and every project type might be unique, which is something that seems logical but has not yet been proven with AI tools. Because this is a supervised learning method, each dataset is labeled either as a project success, 1, or not a success, 0. Based on the input, the machine learning algorithm builds a model that represents the data. The next step is to present a new dataset to see what category it falls in, success or failure, which is expressed as a probability.

Table 3: Typical Machine Learning Input

	Feature 1	Feature 2	Feature 3	Feature 4	Feature ...	Label
Project Dataset 1						
Project Dataset 2						
Project Dataset 3						
Project Dataset 4						
Project Dataset ...						

This simple format can be used for many other purposes. For example, the columns can be risk plans for each project and the features can be items in each risk plan. The label can be a measure of success or failure of the risk plans in terms of exceeding the risk budget or creating schedule problems. Similarly, the datasets can be a list of change orders and the features can be a series of specific content that is included or omitted in the change order. In this case, a label can be added to indicate whether or not the change order was implemented successfully as defined by the project manager. These examples highlight the work with data that needs to precede any machine learning model building.

It is important to build a model that reflects your organization and to spend time on use cases and use case definitions. The use cases describe how the user and system will interact to achieve a result. The project manager must be comfortable and confident that the process works and that the machine learning results are beneficial. Spending time on a use case is similar to a project itself where you need to spend a lot of time making sure that the scope statement is complete and accurate. In some situations, after an objective is defined for a machine learning model, a programmer will check the available data and indicate the ability to create an accurate model or not. Once again, this is similar to project management where some projects are clearly not feasible based on the statement of work. The objective and the available data must be aligned to create a successful machine learning algorithm that will produce results for the new project methodology.

Feature engineering is the practice of performing data analytics to make sure that the proper data and the proper amount of data are being used for the machine learning model. Performing data analytics can result in finding similar or dependent data that reduces the value of the individual features. In this case, a sample set of data can be defined that is representative of the whole dataset and does not contain superfluous data simply for the sake of using everything. On the other hand, there may not be sufficient features or data for the features, which creates an inaccurate and unrepresentative model.

A machine learning model that performs prediction uses regression analysis to calculate a value. It is important to distinguish between a binary classification and a probability percentage. Binary values are either 1 or 0, which can result in misleading outcomes. For example, if the regression results in a value of 52 percent, then that value can be shown as a 1 because the value is greater than 50 percent. In a binary system, this indicates that any value between 50 percent and 100 percent has the same meaning, which is very unlikely. The PMO needs to understand how to interpret the probability values and to investigate any tool that produces binary results.

Another mathematical issue is the accuracy of the probability results that are calculated using unbalanced datasets. This means, for example, that most of the datasets being fed to the model have the same label. If 99 percent of the datasets are labeled with a successful result, then it is difficult for the model to assume anything different. The question becomes: How balanced does the dataset need to be? There is no standard way that will resolve the problem of determining if the model is a good fit for the data. Mathematicians perform analysis of variance (also known as ANOVA) using several statistical models, such as standard deviation. For machine learning algorithms, some mathematicians suggest using the F-test to analyze variance for unbalanced datasets. The F score is a measure of a test's accuracy and measures the precision of the results, which is the degree to which they are clustered tightly as opposed to being scattered. The purpose of this explanation is not to become an expert in statistics but to understand whether the machine learning tool accurately represents the data that is being used to create the model.

Unsupervised learning is used to detect similar patterns in datasets and has the machine learning algorithm group them together, which is known as clustering (see table 4). It is used in data mining to help understand the data. In project management, the clusters can be profiled to identify common attributes, and if datasets are tightly grouped, it might indicate the likelihood of similar events happening in a project. As mentioned at the start of the book, different risks have a high probability of occurring in the same project.

Table 4: Unsupervised Learning Analyzes Data with No Labels

	Feature 1	Feature 2	Feature 3	Feature 4	Feature ...
Project Dataset 1					
Project Dataset 2					
Project Dataset 3					
Project Dataset 4					
Project Dataset ...					

The output results in a grouping of the datasets based on attributes, as shown in figure 4. The machine learning algorithm creates a model that represents this cluster and can now be used for a new dataset to determine which cluster is most representative.

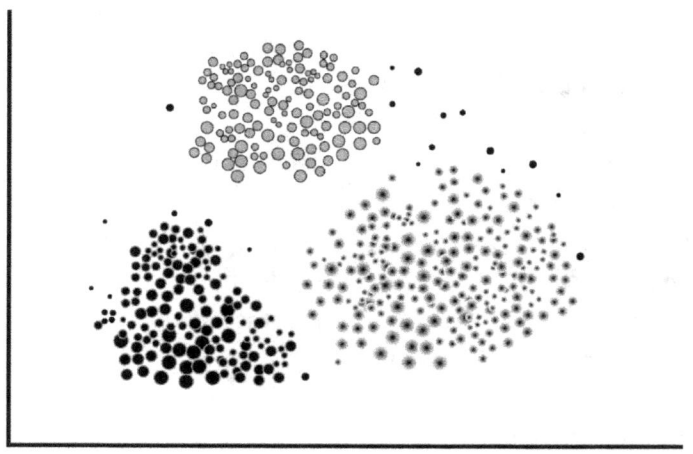

Figure 4: Dataset Clustering

INTERPRET MACHINE LEARNING RESULTS PROPERLY

The PMO needs to understand the limitations of AI as well as the opportunities. For example, interpreting NLP outcomes can be more difficult than simple prediction or classification results. The same statistical models are used in the background, but the data in the form of utterances and emotions can be more open to interpretation. It is not necessarily the results themselves that will create problems but the action taken based on the results. If a stakeholder makes disparaging remarks and continually annoys project team members, then there must be careful consideration of the tactics to use to resolve the situation. If action is taken to resolve a situation that does not truly exist, the project team will become skeptical of AI tools and the AI tools will lose credibility. If a problem is evident and an incorrect response is suggested by AI tools, then this results in the same concerns mentioned previously. At least by using AI tools for sentiment analysis, any issues will be recognized in a timelier manner.

At the early stages of AI implementation, it will be important to validate the results with personal observation. If the AI tool discovers a problem before it is visible, then questions can be asked to verify that the issue exists before any action is taken. Having an AI tool discover stakeholder or project team personal issues is likely to cause frustration, skepticism, and concern. This is an area that will need careful PMO guidance and transparency. In addition, decisions need to be made on the level of analysis that is being performed. For example, should sentiment analysis results be reported on an individual basis or a group basis? Reporting and taking actions based on the analysis of an individual can have significant repercussions. The project team members might become intimidated or try to refrain from providing data to analyze. A more appropriate level is at the group level, where group interactions can be assessed and group sentiment can be reported in summary form. Another alternative is to perform the individual analysis but to provide the feedback results only to the individuals. This might bring forth self-correction.

In any case, this reflects a new level of the invasion of AI into the lives of workers. A marketing website like Amazon may know our personality traits from interactions, but it will be different if this data is used as a productivity tool in the workplace and to improve project performance. In the marketing arena, the more data the computer learns about you, the better it can meet your needs. In the work environment, AI tools may have the ability to propel, halt, modify, or change the trajectory of your career.

MACHINE LEARNING LIMITATIONS

Machine learning is not the answer for every question, nor is it the solution for every problem. If the solution is simple, then it does not make sense to go through all the work to create a machine learning algorithm. One example is where items on a higher shelf are purchased less frequently, probably because customers find the effort too difficult, especially elderly people. The solution is to discount those goods or offer more bonus shopping points that make it worth the effort. There is no need to create an algorithm to find the cause and create a solution if it is easy to determine. In addition, if there is no data or insufficient data available to feed the machine learning tool, then it will be difficult to perform training and make it useful.

The next issue is the risk of deploying an AI tool, something that should be familiar to project managers and the PMO. If the consequences of failure, known as the risk impact in project management language, are extremely negative, then a machine learning tool is not the best option. There is too much risk to hope that an AI tool can solve insurmountable problems, regardless of the tool developed. An example of this occurs when an algorithm is fed real-time data while the results are required instantly or a few minutes later and the latency or speed of the results actually takes much longer. Another issue is the cost for large, complex models that require a lot of data and computing power. The cost might overwhelm the benefit, so the PMO must understand how the scale of the project benefit compares to the cost. In other words, a series of large projects, such as building several hydro-dams, can justify a high cost, but it may not be worthwhile for a simple software system version upgrade.

AI tools are not good at abstraction and have no common sense. A robot can learn to move around a wall but does not know what a wall is. If the wall is made of thin fabric drapery, the robot does not understand that the drapery can be moved aside to go directly through it. The most common example is that AI does not know how to answer the question "Will an elephant fit through a door?"[20] Similarly, AI does not know if a bicycle is alive. These simple commonsense questions are easy for humans, but AI tools cannot solve them (yet). Therefore, it makes no sense to install AI tools where commonsense solutions are the most obvious alternative. This is the AI paradox. AI is significantly smarter than humans in many areas but cannot solve simple problems that humans easily understand. AI tools cannot solve impossible problems, and if solutions create a large risk, it will only decrease the credibility of a valuable technology.[21] Implementing AI tools successfully is important in order to build confidence in the technology. It will take time, and some mistakes will be made. However, it is also important to avoid attempts to implement AI tools where the probability of success is very low. The PMO needs to understand the limitations of AI as well as the potential.

---

20   "Is a Bicycle Alive? Can an Elephant Fit through a House Door? DARPA to Teach AI 'Common Sense,'" RT News, October 14, 2018, https://www.rt.com/news/441237-darpa-ai-common-sense.

21   Daniel Shapiro, "AI Gap Analysis" (lecture, Machine Learning and Artificial Intelligence Ottawa, Ontario, CA, October, 28, 2019).

WHAT IS MACHINE LEARNING GOOD AT?

There are many capabilities of machine learning algorithms, and they can be categorized into a few deployable opportunities. The first is where a human performs a simple task and it cannot be automated with normal software tools. A typical example is to count the number of buildings in a city that are more than three stories tall. A machine learning algorithm can capture images and be trained to recognize the specific requirement. The next category where machine learning excels is for tasks that are too complex for humans and where there is a huge amount of data available. An example is predicting the amount of rainfall in a specific region. To predict the amount of rainfall, a lot of historical data is needed, and humans use less accurate statistics, such as averages or ranges. A machine learning tool, on the other hand, can incorporate a multitude of different factors to arrive at a more accurate prediction.

The third category is for tasks that are well-defined processes and that require decisions based on available data. This is where self-driving vehicles fit. The process to drive a car has a lot of rules and driving techniques, but there is no ambiguity. If the machine learning algorithm can be trained to make good decisions, then this task can be performed more consistently and better than humans. There are other tasks that we don't realize are rules based, and programs based on machine learning can accomplish them. For example, NLP is capable of creating an abstract summary from a document that is thousands of words long without human involvement.[22] This is very applicable to project management processes because a lot of project processes are rules based. Researchers such as myself are scouring these processes to identify the

---

22 Sandeep Subramanian, Raymond Li, Jonathan Pilault, and Christopher Pal, "On Extractive and Abstractive Neural Document Summarization with Transformer Language Models," Cornell University, September 7, 2019, https://arxiv.org/abs/1909.03186.

rules-based project management processes to find ways to develop an AI tool that can perform the activity.

SUMMARY

As with any technology, there are limitations as well as opportunities, and the PMO needs to clearly understand both. There is a sequential process for using machine learning tools, including the access to a structured dataset, validation of the data, preprocessing, model creation, model testing, and the interpretation and use of the results. A machine learning algorithm can process and analyze far more data than a human, and the PMO must take advantage of this capability. It is important to understand the process and the basic concepts so that the result is credible. The result can be interpreted in different ways and can be used for different purposes. Therefore, the PMO needs to be familiar with both the limitations of AI tools and the areas where they excel. It is unlikely that there will be a single comprehensive AI tool that solves all project management issues, and an explanation of that is the topic for the next chapter.

CHAPTER 6:
The Ultimate Machine Learning Algorithm

The survival of project-based organizations depends on a new project methodology powered by artificial intelligence.

In his book *The Master Algorithm*, Pedro Domingos describes the potential for a single unifying algorithm that can learn everything about the world and the people in it.[23] Current AI is only "smarter" than humans in many narrow fields where it can process more information and make much better decisions than humans. At this time, there is no known path of research that will result in a general intelligence machine, which suggests that more breakthroughs in research are required.

THE UNIFIED ALGORITHM

Can there be a single project management machine learning model? The current project management software landscape is dominated by tools that perform project scheduling and workflow management. In the face of AI development, these tools are outdated, and as much as the owners attempt to add pieces of AI to their tools, it is more likely that a completely new tool is required. None of the current vendor software has machine learning at their core or central capability. They follow the older, rules-based pattern of trying to incorporate every branch of possible scenarios into the code. An example is the existing scheduling tools that have a lot of logic and verification capability but little to no machine learning embedded in the steps. Yes, we need scheduling tools, but they have stagnated in the ability to give us a solution that increases the probability for project success. They might suggest a more efficient approach, but generally, they simply provide metrics that show that the project is running late or overspending. A true machine learning tool needs to proactively work to produce successful results instead of describing metrics that represent the beginning of project failure. The existing project management software is driving the proliferation of new project management capability that uses AI technology. However, none of the tools contain a unified

---

23 Domingos, *The Master Algorithm*.

machine learning algorithm, which is undoubtedly a tough challenge. The foundation for a unified algorithm has to be a holistic approach to managing projects, very similar to what is expected from a project manager.

Perhaps it is a series of layered machine learning algorithms coupled with rules-based software that creates a way to manage a project similar to the self-driving car analogy. This type of solution has machine learning concepts at the core and analyzes the project environment using a series of rules for driving a project as well as decisions that are based on machine learning models. The major difference in a project environment is that the tools try to predict issues before they happen. The ultimate AI tool finds ways to resolve problems at the beginning of the project, as well as throughout the project, before they cause a negative impact to the results. The predictor tool finds probabilities and helps in the decision-making process. The predictor tool concept can also be incorporated into an ultimate tool to provide guidance, but the ultimate AI tool is one that proactively resolves project problems as a main function. Of course, there must be another function that deals with problems in real time because projects inevitably encounter unpredictable problems. Before the self-driving project starts its engine, there are aspects to project management that need to be reviewed and understood.

Many project managers who lack formal training in project management are not even aware of the concept of a critical path or the value of understanding it when evaluating project activities. In addition, most existing tools focus on a few areas of managing a project and ignore other critical areas, such as risk, quality, or communications. A comprehensive machine learning tool must consider a holistic perspective of the project. It needs to go beyond the critical path and use machine learning technology as the essential element that considers every activity and drives every decision. To do this, the tool needs to start with the project activity list. This is derived from the work breakdown structure (WBS) but includes the dependencies.

There are additional attributes that need to be attached to each activity. Specifically, these include risk, quality, resources, interrelationship with other projects, and cost. Also, from an overall project perspective, there is a communications plan, a stakeholder management plan, and the possibility of procurement, where tasks or materials are provided by a vendor. While these might have items related to specific activities, there will also be an overall strategy. The challenge is to create a machine learning tool that can be used for each activity as well as the overall plans. However, as a machine learning model is designed for specific activities, there must be a separate one that considers all aspects of project management.

For example, in table 5, an analysis of Activity 1 uses a machine learning algorithm to verify the cost estimate and schedule duration based on the model created from historical data. In addition, the model can identify risk attached to this activity as well as typical quality results, if applicable. The model can either identify the proper resources or whether an assigned resource is adequate. These assessments are ideally performed before or at the start of the project.

Table 5: Activity Attribute Table

WBS ID	Activity Name	Predecessors	Logical Relationship	Lead/Lag
1	Activity 1	None	FS	0
1.1	Activity 1.1	1	FS	0
2	Activity 2	1.1	FS	0
3	Activity 3	1,2	FS	0

Project activities also must be analyzed using the theory of constraints (TOC).[24] This concept is used to analyze data to identify any bottlenecks that can delay a project. While the TOC has been used extensively in operations environments, there are elements that can be adapted to project management. It is normal to think about tasks on the critical path as the cause for project slippage, but any task can be delayed if it encounters a bottleneck. A bottleneck could be a piece of equipment or an expert resource that has limited availability. This is a difficult area for a machine learning tool because the data is most likely to be buried inside the project performance data and not easily evident. However, if provided with the appropriate data, AI can predict the appearance of a bottleneck that threatens the success of a project. Once identified, steps need to be taken to eliminate either the bottleneck or the probability of occurrence. In essence, this becomes a risk that must be managed, and it is best to manage it prior to the event happening.

There should be an analysis of overall project risk, even though risk events are mainly related to an individual task or to a series of tasks. If you are building a road and the ground collapses under it, then a series of tasks will be delayed. A machine learning tool is able to assess risk at both a project level and a task level. For example, individual tasks can be evaluated to see if they fall within the parameters of cost and schedule, based on historical data from similar projects. To achieve quality goals, a machine learning algorithm can perform data mining on historical project data to determine the correlations that cause poor or unacceptable quality. There is always a factor or several factors that result in achieving the quality objectives for a project. The factors will be revealed by using AI tools, because with sufficient examination of the data, the truth will be exposed.

---

24 Eli Goldratt, *Critical Chain: Project Management and the Theory of Constraints* (Prince Frederick, MD: HighBridge, 2014), audiobook.

Communication will no longer be a generic strategy when using a unified algorithm. Machine learning tools can build a personal profile for every project stakeholder, which takes all factors into consideration, including personality types, emotional states, communication methods, and personal goals. Communication from the ultimate machine learning tool will consider all relevant data and will deliver a customized message that resonates with each person. If that sounds scary, it probably is. The message will start with a hook to grab the attention of each person and continue with content that is presented in a way that has the best possibility to connect with a receptive part of our mind. Based on historical personal data, an AI program will excel at communication.

The current machine learning tools are mainly based on supervised learning, which uses labeled datasets to make correlations. The next development in machine learning is to train a model using unsupervised learning—that is, having the algorithm develop knowledge of a project by gathering every piece of data as the project progresses. This is similar to building a corpus for project management language, but this time it is building knowledge about project management decisions and daily issues that occur along the way. From that data, the algorithm can build an image of what project management logic is; from there, a project can be labeled a success or failure and the algorithm can learn from that data.

The most difficult part is applying updated logic to a project. This is because machines are particularly inept at reading and interpreting project management concepts. When an issue arises, perhaps the algorithm will simply see successful decisions and recommend a similar solution without even understanding why the issue exists. This is similar to the creation of success for the AlphaGo game, where the computer has to play numerous games before it understands how to achieve the best results. Once it identifies the best model or strategy, the tool makes decisions that would result in achieving as close as possible to the winning formula. If this approach is successful, it will eventually allow the PMO to hand over project control to AI tools.

CREATING THE SINGLE SOLUTION

One method to create an all-encompassing project management AI tool is to use the philosophy of learning from a game, such as the results achieved by AlphaGo or AlphaZero. In a research study, the use of project management games improved player decision-making ability. It also discovered that the complexity of the games did not impair the performance.[25] The AlphaGo solution combines machine learning algorithms with the Monte Carlo technique that assesses values on decision trees. It also performs a limited amount of preprocessing to detect patterns. To train the tool, it first has to learn the rules of the game, which, in our case, means the basic principles of project management. Next, it must play a variety of project management simulators or be fed project data that occurs as the project is being executed.

An alternative is to train the algorithm based on project management theory and successful decisions, without using historical datasets. The purpose of this strategy is based on AlphaZero development where the tool was considered more powerful because it was not constrained by human knowledge.[26] In other words, there were no limits to what options the tools could select, whereas project managers are normally constrained by their own project experience as well as by how much knowledge they have about project management concepts.

---

25 David Rumeser and Margaret Emsley, "Can Serious Games Improve Project Management Decision Making under Complexity?" *PMI Journal* 50, no. 5 (2019): 23–39.

26 David Silver, Thomas Hubert, Julian Schrittwieser, and Demis Hassabis, "AlphaZero: Shedding New Light on Chess, Shogi, and Go," DeepMind, December 6, 2018, https://deepmind.com/blog/article/alphazero-shedding-new-light-grand-games-chess-shogi-and-go.

Collecting real-time data from a project will be challenging. There must be a focus on project changes as they occur, what decisions or actions are taken as a result of any new information, and the results or outcome of the actions taken.

The goal for data collection is to capture project documents at the start of a project and to collect data as the project is being executed. Changes from project databases must also be monitored, such as variance to scope, test plans, risks, and so on. Is it possible to perform real-time data mining to uncover changes made that are not approved or work that was done that was not performed correctly? This goes beyond simply capturing data and into understanding why a change happened, then including it as a learning moment for an AI tool.

One of the most important characteristics of good project managers is that they are proactive. When something is happening that will create issues, such as a delay in the project schedule or an increase in spending, the project manager looks for possibilities to make a correction. AI tools exist today that perform the same proactive steps. Think about typing a word into a smartphone. Before you finish typing the word, the phone suggests what your word will be. Similarly, on websites like LinkedIn, when someone you know sends a message or is celebrating an event, the system will suggest such responses as "Good work" or "Congrats on your work anniversary." These are simple examples of AI tools being proactive to help an individual, and we must use the same concepts to anticipate and find responses to issues in project management.

The first step is the Amazon approach. An Amazon algorithm recommends items for you to buy based on your profile; similarly, an AI tool for project management must be able to suggest several possible actions to remedy a project problem. Using machine learning algorithms, this can then be narrowed down to the best solution. This also highlights the problem with piecemeal solutions. If a person is trying to complete a task and is spending more time than estimated, an AI tool might suggest that they be replaced or that you need to add resources. Using common sense, you might think that the best solution is to allow the employee to work through the issues in order to increase their learning so that they can carry that to future tasks. Also, this person might be a leader who other team members respect, and replacing them or adding help can be humiliating and result in the opposite of what is trying to be achieved.

USING THE ULTIMATE ALGORITHM

The ultimate AI tool will be embedded with an intelligent agent that can be accessed using verbal (chatbot) or written communication. This is likely to be more than a single machine learning algorithm and might be similar to creating general intelligence, which is too much work to initiate simply to replace a project manager. The purpose of the intelligent agent is to understand all aspects of the project and to make decisions that will optimize the project outcomes, mainly the success in terms of delivering the scope, on schedule and within budget. It requires that the tool is linked to all organizational systems, including any systems that are specific to the project. For example, if a team member makes a minor change to a document or an architectural drawing without a change order or approval, then the AI tool will know. The minor change might be the initial creation of larger problems as the project progresses. Remember that the project manager is the person who has the total perspective of the project, so it is not unusual for a team member to see a change as minor in their own context when it actually has more severe repercussions. The intelligent agent requires access to all the data; therefore, this change is one piece of data that the AI tool can consider immediately, whereas the project manager may not find out until the actual problem occurs much later in the project.

In addition to having access to all internal data, the intelligent agent must access environmental and organizational data. The solution is likely to be a series of algorithms, as previously mentioned. The algorithms need to be based on discovering data that helps a project succeed and not necessarily on project management best practices. Academics continue to attempt to identify best practices, when the new reality is that the data will determine what is best for each project or for each organization. The AI tool must understand the situation and all the possibilities, but it should make decisions based on data, not on hard-coded rules. Rules imply that there is only one logical solution to each issue while with AI tools we are looking for a high-probability decision based on current and historical data. An example of this occurs when a task is taking much longer than originally planned, so the project manager adds a resource to help. That might be the obvious solution and can be a rule for a software program to include. However, an AI tool can try to uncover the reason for the additional effort. Is there an unidentified risk? Is it a unique occurrence, or will other tasks similar to this also take more time? There is a myriad of possibilities, so the idea that only a rules-based solution will work is presumptuous.

Having made this argument, an intelligent agent still needs to be able to understand project management logic. The agent must know the concept of a critical path and, for agile projects, that customers should be continuously updated and provided feedback for each sprint. Whether it is a unified algorithm or an intelligent agent that becomes available for project management, there is no doubt that it is required. Most executives understand the importance of deploying AI tools and this includes those in project-based organizations. Survival in a competitive environment depends on a new project methodology powered by artificial intelligence.[27]

---

[27] Jonathan Vanian, "Most Executives Fear Their Companies Will Fail if They Don't Adopt A.I.," *Fortune*, November 14, 2019, https://fortune.com/2019/11/14/executives-fear-accenture-a-i.

SUMMARY

There is no single algorithm (yet) that solves all problems and is capable of making all decisions. To create an ultimate machine learning tool, there must be a comprehensive systems approach that links access to databases in real time, has sufficient hardware components, and is regularly supported and updated. For project management, a comprehensive AI tool needs to understand complex concepts, such as the critical path and the theory of constraints. Training of an AI tool can be performed in a traditional supervised learning approach with labeled data or perhaps by treating project management as a game and learning by repeatedly playing the game in order to learn the rules and to achieve the best outcome. The most likely form of a comprehensive tool will be an intelligent agent that can be accessed by either verbal or written communication. Although the likelihood of an ultimate AI tool for project management is very low, the purpose of this investigation is to uncover more detail about how any AI project management tool will be constructed and used. In fact, the next chapter tries to compile a series of algorithms into a single method to manage a project.

CHAPTER 7
The Self-Driving Project

AI will surpass all expectations once it is integrated properly into the new project methodology.

This best approach to changing the process methodology is to be disruptive in the way that projects are managed, and this deserves a detailed review so that areas for improvement are highlighted and bottom-line improvement opportunities are identified. In other words, the process needs to be performed differently to get the greatest value. While making changes to the individual components is a safe way to begin, careful consideration must be given to a more comprehensive or holistic approach, which means that individual changes must be properly integrated into the overall project methodology. Many project components overlap or interact, and making a small change in one area might have an unintended negative impact on another area of the project. Certainly, the culture of the organization has an impact on the ability to make changes, and the PMO needs to evaluate and increase the maturity level in terms of project awareness, standards, metrics, and acceptance of change. In fact, there are AI tools that can help in this process too.

The analogy of a self-driving car is a good model to use when thinking about how to create a self-driving project. There is a lot of work for preparation, there is a clear destination, and there is a series of events during the journey. The preparation, or planning as it is called in project management, often determines the success of the journey. Having a self-driving project offers incredible cost reduction. Even if it provides only a 30 percent improvement, this results in significant savings to costs and resource usage. The self-driving project must be able to manage any problems encountered along the way. For example, problems such as schedule compression and resource utilization are managed with rules-based solutions that are easily programmed using normal software tools. Can software that contains extensive logic be combined with machine learning algorithms to achieve a successful project outcome and improve the bottom line? Let's begin the journey.

PREPARING

Preparation for a project starts with an approved project charter that defines the goals and objectives of the project and includes acceptance criteria, which are the set of metrics used to evaluate project completion and the outcome. The acceptance criteria become the set of metrics that helps guide the project and are used in making decisions. The planning stage of the project begins with the creation of numerous project documents, and AI tools assist with this responsibility. NLP is used to ensure that complete and accurate documents are created. A more accurate scope statement influences other plans, such as the project schedule and resource allocation, and can have a dramatic positive impact during the project executing, or driving, stage. The documents include, but are not limited to, the scope statement, the project schedule, the project budget, the resource plan, the risk register, the quality management plan, and the communications plan.

A self-driving project using a machine learning tool can be trained to recognize a comprehensive scope statement that will result in a higher probability of project success. For software development projects, a tool like ScopeMaster is an excellent choice to verify the scope and to identify errors or inconsistencies. This is especially useful because finding and correcting errors at this early stage of the project is extremely valuable. We know in software projects that finding errors or omissions during a later stage, such as user acceptance testing, can lead to increased cost and significant delays in the project. Finding them at the early stages is a tremendous benefit. ScopeMaster uses NLP as well as other modules to analyze written documents. An added benefit to organizations is that finding potential bugs and performing scope cost estimates can be an educational tool that helps people learn how to create accurate scope definitions. In fact, in the self-driving project, the AI tools scour all project documents for anomalies. These can be based on previous similar internal projects, NLP-based interpretation, or the external environment—if that type of data is available. External data might include economic conditions, industry factors, government regulations, available resource skills, or competitive factors. The purpose of spending effort on a complete and accurate scope statement is to avoid or minimize scope problems that are likely to occur later in the project.

For any project, creating a comprehensive statement of work is normally based on a previous similar project and updated for the specific differences in the current project. The scope is reviewed with the project sponsor or customer and any negotiation is managed by an AI virtual project manager. The schedule and budget are created based on historical data. Once the duration and budget are calculated, a project predictor tool is used to predict the probability of project success. With a reasonable probability, the project proceeds. If not, the AI tool will search for a correlation that needs to be adjusted in the project plans. The remaining project documents are created by the AI tool and an expert system using historical data. The expert system is used to create actual documents in a proper format. These documents include the risk register, the quality plan, the resource requirements, the communications plan, and the stakeholder management plan.

An important consideration in planning is to understand how the project fits in the portfolio with other projects. One of the central responsibilities of a PMO is to coordinate projects across the organization. The PMO has a high-level view and should be the owner of interactions, dependencies, and potential conflicts. On an individual project basis, this usually means that one project must complete a task so that the next project can continue or that a project must be completed so that resources can be moved immediately to another project. The dependencies can be common resources or the results from a deliverable. Typically, these links are not captured or stored as a separate requirement and often show up as project issues or risks. How will the self-driving project manage these links and provide value to the PMO?

The first step is for an AI tool to identify the links and then classify them as a risk that the PMO can manage. Also, an AI tool can use historical data to uncover dependencies with other projects that might be missing or not previously considered. This involves data mining project management plans as well as project status data. Having AI manage dependencies will be one of the more difficult processes to implement and should not be the first AI tool to consider. However, the value to the PMO can be significant if these dependencies can be managed in a way that avoids negative consequences and brings consistent improvement across the project portfolio landscape.

The largest dependency is normally resources that move from one project to another after a project is complete. On some occasions, this occurs during the project execution phase or on a temporary or loan basis. As mentioned previously, a tool like Epicflow helps assign and manage resources across multiple projects, understanding the constraints and critical path of each project. In my experience, the most common problem is having a project unable to start on time because a resource from a different project was delayed and the resource was needed longer. This can be a frustrating experience, especially when there is no advance warning of the project delay, but it is also something that AI tools can predict with greater accuracy. Effective scheduling software is able to manage these issues across a portfolio, and if the complexity is high and unexpected problems plague the organization, then a machine learning tool can be used to understand the relationships.

As part of the self-driving project preparation, the project success predictor tool is used to determine the probability of success based on the project documents.[28] To receive approval to proceed, it will be the responsibility of the PMO to insist that new projects include the prediction factor. If the probability of success is considered to be too low,

---

28   See chapter 3.

further action can be taken by the PMO. As the process is repeated for many projects, this will become a good practice for the organization because all projects will be evaluated to a common standard. With reinforcement learning used as feedback to update the algorithm, projects will be evaluated to a higher standard and become more successful.

AI tools are used to acquire and assign resources by classifying the skills required, then reviewing the availability of employees who have the ability to complete the required tasks. With a limited pool of skilled resources, the AI tool evaluates the use of external resources, in addition to internal resources, in an attempt to optimize the results. Similar to normal projects, the solution might be to adequately staff the project, as opposed to acquiring team members with above-average skills. In many situations, the resource assignment will be obvious, but there will be activities where there is some uncertainty as to the best choice. These are excellent decisions for a machine learning algorithm, where the budget, schedule, risk, and quality are all assessed with sufficient quantifiable data to develop a clear decision.

Something to note as the self-driving project continues in the preparation stage is that AI tools do not replace existing project management tools. They augment them by mining for data and improving the accuracy and reliability of the results. However, AI tools can replace analytics tools or simulation software and perform the same functions. The advantage of an AI tool is the cognitive capability, which means a better decision can be made and allow the self-driving project to move forward without the help of a driver (i.e., project manager).

The final step in the preparation stage is to make sure that there is a project manager or a PMO person who is trained in how to use the AI tools. Some results may need interpretation, or common sense might be needed where an AI tool gets stuck. Even the first self-driving cars had drivers (called safety drivers) who made sure to monitor the surroundings.[29]

EXECUTING

As the self-driving car starts its journey, it is flooded with real-time data used for feedback to make sure that it obeys the rules of the road. The car must drive within the speed limit, stay in its lane, understand location data, make course adjustments based on the destination, and adhere to traffic regulations, such as stopping at a stop sign. For a self-driving project, the ongoing data includes the monitoring of project status. Compared to the volume of data fed to the algorithms in the self-driving car, the project status data is likely to be insufficient and fragmented in the early stages. To make this scenario a reality, there must be a greater focus on project control data.

One of the first responsibilities is to hold a project kickoff meeting. An AI tool can create the information slide deck based on critical project information in the project documents as well as on who will be attending the meeting. For a virtual team meeting, an AI voice and the content presented might be indistinguishable from that of a real human.[30] The information is presented and the AI asks for feedback and answers any questions. Similar to a virtual assistant, AI achieves this by accessing documents, organizational policies and procedures, and environmental data. Any questions that cannot be answered by the AI tool can be referred to the PMO.

Similar to a self-driving car, the self-driving project has rules-based approaches that can be taken for several events. For example, if a risk

---

29 Stan Horaczek, "The Role of Humans in Self-Driving Cars Is Even More Complicated after Uber's Fatal Crash," *Popular Science*, March 23, 2018, https://www.popsci.com/human-drivers-and-self-driving-car.

30 Google Duplex, "A.I. Assistant Calls Local Businesses to Make Appointments," YouTube, May 8, 2018, https://www.youtube.com/watch?v=D5VN56jQMWM.

occurs, then the risk response is implemented. Unlike the self-driving car, the self-driving project is likely to encounter numerous unanticipated events, such as a scope change request, a late material delivery, or a resource that leaves the project before their work is complete. However, the self-driving car learns responses over time and with training. If a stop sign is bent over and the self-driving car cannot detect the image, then it evaluates other data, such as the post in the ground at an intersection and the likelihood that a stop is required. This happens in projects as well and we call it project management experience. The problem is accessing structured data from a repository of all project management experience for every project completed. A lack of data for the self-driving project is a serious issue, but machine learning tools can improve over time with project experience.

Managing a change to scope has already been discussed, and a machine learning tool can find the optimal solution for implementing the change, then continue with the project. For schedule concerns, reducing the project duration or recovering schedule slippage is known as schedule compression and is performed by either schedule crashing or fast tracking. Both of these methods are rules-based approaches. Schedule crashing identifies the least costly way to improve the schedule, which is done by adding resources. Fast tracking finds activities that can be performed in parallel instead of sequentially with the lowest additional risk. The fast tracking technique can maintain a finish-to-start dependency but allows a dependent task to start before the previous one ends for situations where this is acceptable.

As the self-driving project continues, the spending data against the budget is captured and EVM metrics are calculated based on task completion and costs. Because this is rules based, EVM metrics can be continually updated. For budget concerns, the first step is to identify which costs on the project are fixed and which are variable. The machine learning algorithm can determine the best opportunity to reduce variable costs, by how much, and with minimal impact to the project objectives. The important consideration with EVM metrics and spending in general is to detect a trend and to address the issue as soon as possible. The best project managers are proactive, and the self-driving project needs to adopt that strategy. As the collection of data on spending by task occurs, it is fed to other self-driving projects. They can then use the data to develop more accurate project budgets and to analyze issues with resource efficiency within time and cost constraints.

How does the self-driving project that is based on AI reduce costs on a project that already has an approved project budget? One method to look at is the cost estimates that use the three-point method for creating a cost estimate. In a three-point cost estimate, three factors are considered for an activity: the optimistic estimate, the most likely estimate, and the pessimistic estimate. The AI tool reduces the budget cost for an activity by evaluating what needs to be done to achieve the optimistic cost. The self-driving project identifies the conditions that permit tasks to be completed at the optimistic estimate and implements those conditions.

Issues concerning a lack of resources occur during any project, at any time. If something happens to a project team member, the self-driving project handles the information so that it is always ready with a list of alternatives. Considerations are made for an internal replacement, a contractor, or a temporary worker. Although this is thought of typically as a project manager making a detailed evaluation and then making a decision, it is mainly rules based, with the most important element being access to data. Because a machine learning tool can access and analyze more data, it is likely that the self-driving project will make a better decision, or at least a faster decision, than a human project manager.

In terms of project processes for procurement, there are many reasons why an organization selects a vendor to complete projects. In this situation, how are machine learning algorithms applied? The organization can still use their own algorithms to assess the probability of success either for the scope statement or based on the vendor's project documents. Also, data mining can be used to determine whether an RFP is complete before being sent to potential vendors. The organization can add evaluation criteria to the responses, seeking data on the vendor's plan for using AI tools on the project and any past results they can show based on similar work. What happens when an organization and a vendor have a dispute, for example, regarding a discrepancy in scope? If the issue cannot be resolved with facts from an agreed scope statement or from wording in the contract, then the project manager may be required to negotiate. Fortunately for the self-driving project, AI tools are advancing to a state where they are overtaking humans in the ability to negotiate.[31]

Projects inevitably run into problems, and the self-driving project must be able to solve them at least as well as a project manager. Problem-solving has several steps that make it a candidate for a rules-based approach. After communicating the issue to the appropriate stakeholders, one of the usual steps for a serious problem is to hold a meeting. The intent of the meeting is to bring in experts and project team members to have a discussion of alternatives, select the best alternative, and implement the resolution or an interim action. However, AI itself is an expert and has access to more data and can analyze the data better than humans. The exception is where there is insufficient data or the problem is so unique that finding an effective solution is difficult. In that situation, the AI tool evaluates all alternatives based on input and creates a probability assessment of which options are likely to be more successful.

---

31 Matthew Hutson, "How Artificial Intelligence Could Negotiate Better Deals for Humans," *Science Magazine*, September 11, 2017, https://www.sciencemag.org/news/2017/09/how-artificial-intelligence-could-negotiate-better-deals-humans.

There is a misguided belief that AI cannot be creative. This is important because project managers feel that creative solutions are frequently required to resolve project issues. An example of creativity is how the AI-based IBM Watson platform was used to develop a movie trailer.[32] Other AI tools have created paintings and written works. There is a process to human creativity, such as lateral thinking, and while AI tools are not at human level yet, they probably have enough creativity currently to solve a majority of project problems.

Managing risks is also a rules-based activity. Once the risk register and risk plan are created, they determine the sequence of steps for risk events in the project. For example, if a risk occurs, then the risk response is initiated. Once the response and the activity associated with the risk are complete, then an AI tool can analyze data for any residual risks. Residual risks only occur because the initial risk happened and are not normally predictable during risk planning. A residual or secondary risk goes through the same process as a normal risk and is added to the risk register with an analysis of the probability of occurrence, the impact on the project, and a risk response. As activities are completed, and the associated risks are no longer a possibility, the contingency fund set aside for risks is highlighted as available based on the project budget and, of course, the organizational policies.

MANAGING COMMUNICATION

From an informal poll that I created on ProjectManager.com, 43 percent of respondents thought that governance and communication should be the primary responsibility of a PMO. In addition, 65 percent believed that communication was the most important skill for

---

32 John R. Smith, "IBM Research Takes Watson to Hollywood with the First 'Cognitive Movie Trailer,'" IBM, August 31, 2016, https://www.ibm.com/blogs/think/2016/08/cognitive-movie-trailer.

successful project managers. AI tools to improve communication are already being implemented in organizations, and PMOs can find a way to adapt these tools for project environments.

For a self-driving project, ongoing attention must be given to managing project communication as this is often cited as a reason for project failure. Typically, if the organization already uses AI tools as part of the communication strategy, the self-driving project can take advantage of the existing process. As the project is progressing, an AI tool accesses organizational emails, instant messages, and possibly verbal communications in order to evaluate whether project sentiment is favorable or unfavorable. This type of analysis, using NLP, can verify or change proposed action plans and strategies to manage project team members and other project stakeholders. With a sentiment analysis tool, it is possible to detect changes in the level of stakeholder engagement and to recommend corrective actions. This is valuable information for a self-driving project. For example, when receiving early feedback that a stakeholder who was previously positive is now resistant to project implementation, the tool can assess the seriousness of a concern and whether it is a valid problem for the project. An AI tool can determine the response that is the most effective in managing each individual's concerns.

The purpose of managing communication is to proactively address stakeholder concerns and to find ways to motivate project team members. An AI tool can recommend the best communication style for each stakeholder based on their personality profile. An AI tool accomplishes this by identifying personality characteristics, performing sentiment analysis based on verbal or written communication, and then determining how to most effectively communicate a message. This type of tool may seem invasive, but it is already in place now for other purposes. In marketing, consumers are tracked to capture their preferences. Software such as location analytics and facial recognition is used by retailers and mall owners to track and measure customer shopping behavior.[33] Based on communication, NLP can assess satisfaction, stress, and frustration as the project progresses and can provide an opportunity to respond or give feedback immediately rather than wait for worsening conditions. It enables proactive, rather than reactive, action. Also, improved communication based on individual personality is more effective than a generic response. For example, introverts need time to process an input and they prefer to receive prior notification with a clear topic so that they are not surprised. Sentiment analysis using NLP has several more benefits. It validates that the communication process is effective, it determines positive and negative trends across the various stakeholder groups, and it can be used to compare results and trends across the different projects in the organization.

The self-driving project also uses NLP to translate languages, and there are several tools currently available that perform this function. The benefit is that language will no longer be a restriction to the creation of a global team. Project team members can work in their native language and use AI tools to communicate with others. Caution still needs to be taken with regard to culture and the nuances of communication in different counties. It may take time to integrate this tool into a diverse global team, but it offers a breakthrough in team formation and collaboration.

The self-driving project uses a virtual assistant to help promote shared communication and a common understanding among project team members, although there needs to be a control mechanism in place to validate real-time data before it is made available. Real-time data might be incomplete or misinterpreted if it is made instantly available. This type of access to project data supports the concept of ubiquitous project management, where the content of project documents

---

33 Sarah Rieger, "At Least Two Malls Are Using Facial Recognition Technology to Track Shoppers' Ages and Genders without Telling," CBC News, July 27, 2018, https://www.cbc.ca/new/canada/calgary/calgary-malls-1.4760964.

is available anytime and anywhere, which is supportive of a globally dispersed team. To provide feedback to the project team, the self-driving project uses AI to determine the best communication method based on the content and the intended audience. This includes messaging, email, and sending text through a workflow tool, and it can also be verbal by using a virtual assistant similar to Siri or Alexa. A face-to-face conversation is obviously not possible, which might be a gap that needs to be resolved. In spite of many project employees who might prefer electronic communication, a face-to-face meeting can be the most effective method of direct communication, although this may soon become a false assumption. This also assumes that a human is more effective at direct communication, which is not always true.

In the near future, an AI tool such as this will be constantly scanning employee communication and categorizing sentiment to provide clear and timely recommendations on how to address a variety of issues. This capability might become indispensable to the organization. Will the benefits outweigh the privacy concerns?

The next step is to monitor employee actions outside the workplace, which is already in place in several organizations for social media posts. This is implemented legally by creating policies and informing employees. In many cases, there is an expected level of professionalism from employees at all times in public. Think of professional athletes who receive discipline for behaving poorly outside of their normal place of work. Similarly, a project stakeholder can be monitored while engaged in conversations after normal working hours or perhaps even while not discussing work-related activities.

The acceptance of this level of scrutiny will most likely continue to be controversial. The organization needs to work with the PMO to determine what level of sentiment analysis is required or will be permitted. Tracking individuals is effective but it leads to ethical issues. People may not want to work on a project that uses this type of tracking, and those who are not project stakeholders may feel negatively toward this concept. Is it acceptable to have an algorithm read and analyze emails and text messages? Perhaps this would be acceptable for an organization that has an open culture and is determined to have successful project results or for an overbearing organization that wants project success at any cost. There is also a possibility of having microphones in project meetings to capture conversations that can be analyzed by AI tools. In fact, some project meetings are recorded deliberately in order to retain accurate records of decisions. Capturing dialogue, either formal or informal conversations, is considered more invasive and has implications for making an individual feel uncomfortable with verbal communication. This capability reveals the incredible disruption that AI tools will have.

Making the sentiment results anonymous is a more palatable alternative. High-level tracking and summarization of results where the users remain anonymous is less invasive and still provides valuable information, such as the trend of positive or negative feelings toward the progress of the project. For example, a tool would anonymously measure the overall trend of positive to negative feelings toward the progress of the project. Ownership of this type of data produced by AI tools may fall to the PMO, which will have to decide how to use the output. The purpose of this discussion is not to judge the ethics of any organization or AI tool but rather to present the capability that is available.

Based on a person's voice and facial expression, an AI tool can detect stress or a possible medical condition. The potential for sentiment analysis goes significantly beyond positive or negative feelings toward a project. Voice analysis tools will be able to identify when someone is nervous about being able to achieve the end date for a task but does not want to reveal any problems. People who are overly aggressive on goals or claim that they can perform more work than they are capable of accomplishing will be evident to an AI tool. While this may seem invasive to a person's privacy, the ultimate goal is to increase success rates on a project, and competitive pressures demand serious considerations of any possible advantage. Does the result justify the method? If the method provides a positive benefit not only to the project outcome but also to the project manager and the project team members, then it may be easier to accept. People wear Apple Watches and Fitbits to track or maintain a healthy regimen. The goal is to transfer that concept of self-motivation to a project team and to create a more positive environment that in turn will increase the probability of project success. It is possible that the desire to participate in a winning project will outweigh concerns of personal privacy in the work environment.

Technology can be used for purposes other than what they were designed for, which can easily happen in this situation. A self-driving project that selects team members and assigns work might try to replace a team member who is too nervous to analyze and is not forthcoming about problems. There will be additional concerns using AI tools—for example, trying to mold a team into a group whose members are all very driven to succeed could result in either groupthink or irreconcilable conflict. The same tool that has the ability to create a positive and sharing project team environment also has the ability to do the opposite, depending on how the data is used. A person might be having a bad day and not be particularly friendly, and that information should not be made available to other people, organizations, or social media. Who can predict what the implementation of a sentiment analysis tool will look like and how the organization will manage and control the results? It is hoped that the PMO will find a way to achieve the benefits while avoiding the pitfalls.

One of the problems that happens to project managers can also happen to the self-driving project: a team member who simply does not comply with any instructions. Assuming that the AI tool made a proper selection and task assignment, the person may have emotional problems with the organization, the work, or other people. How will AI handle the situation? The first step is to follow organizational procedures and document issues, then perhaps escalate the problem to the

PMO, similar to what is expected from a project manager. Is it appropriate to use an AI tool to find a way to force a poor-performing team member to change? An analysis needs to be performed as to why the person's performance, and possibly their attitude, is unacceptable. The hope is that NLP and AI analysis can uncover root causes and make suggestions to resolve them; I routinely see project managers who are frustrated with this problem and are unable to find a happy resolution.

SUMMARY

The self-driving project does not exist, and it will take more software development and much more data, including capturing data in real time, before this concept becomes a reality. However, the PMO can think of the project process in self-driving terms and put effort into highlighting the tools and data that are needed to move forward. There are many improvements that can be made both by simply observing the journey and by using AI tools to find better ways to resolve issues.

Managing communication is one of the more challenging tasks for a self-driving project and will consequently be a challenge for the PMO in making this effective. An AI tool is a powerful assistant to help with this responsibility, although the process is complex, requiring the ability to understand project management vocabulary and to identify different stakeholder personalities. The result is an output that has the capability to optimize personal interactions on the project or, on the other hand, to create negative emotions. Using NLP-based analysis on people can be invasive, but it can also be rewarding and motivating. To be successful, creative solutions must be developed, including privacy and ethical considerations.

CHAPTER 8
How to Deceive AI Tools

The PMO may be the only group that can balance the benefits and the costs of AI tools.

This chapter should be titled how to *deliberately* fool machine learning algorithms, and it provides insight that is required by the PMO to understand the changes faced by project stakeholders, and especially project team members, when AI tools dominate the workplace. This is a recipe for how workers can alter the output of machine learning algorithms when they have lost faith in the ability to be judged fairly. Some people have an aversion to technology, especially invasive technology, and try to hide or become invisible. That approach is not possible when you are committed to a workplace and trying to develop a career.

MANAGE YOUR PROFILE

If you are a project team member employed by an organization and under constant scrutiny by AI tools, there are ways to enhance your profile and hide your personal information. Dating websites are a good analogy for how to manipulate a personal profile. People use photos and text in their profiles to fool the matching algorithm that is used to make potential matches. Perhaps embellishing one's personal characteristics is considered a good marketing technique and the person is only highlighting their best qualities. On the other hand, some profiles have been known to contain fake photos and even false, or at least exaggerated, personal profile information. It will be important in a workplace that uses AI to find ways to build your profile within the organization. This can be performed by training the AI algorithm with all your good habits and none of your bad ones. AI tools learn from data, so your task is to provide it with the best parts of you. If AI seems to be manipulative or invasive, then these suggestions are only countering any negative implications that a person could face by being themselves and occasionally revealing flaws.

You can build a false profile by leading the tracking information in a certain direction. It won't be difficult at this early stage of AI. Remember when you performed an online search for a specific item, such as a pair of boots, to see different styles and then went to a store and bought them? For the next several weeks, all the online ads you saw were about boots because the tracking system did not get the message that you bought them. This even happens when you actually purchase something online. You search for a new web camera, purchase it online, and still, for the next several weeks, you get ads for web cameras. Maybe the machine learning algorithm thinks you need two? The point is that you can lead a machine learning tool to build a certain profile by deliberately clicking on items that you don't even want.

To enhance your profile, start following groups that align with your organization's goals. For example, following an AI company or a leadership site will show that you have ambition and are willing to learn new skills. Find favorable professionals to connect to and "like" articles without actually reading them. Browse for items that make you appear more professional, such as a new laptop or a store that sells business attire. Don't think about who you want to be. Instead, think about who "they" want you to be and build that profile. Your image can be the young, ambitious, and energetic career professional while your real self just wants to get through work every day and get paid. Building the profile requires that you also avoid certain items. If you are female, do not shop for maternity items online for a baby shower because the tracker will think you are pregnant and an unenlightened boss will start reducing your interesting work in preparation for you to take time off. Everyone needs to avoid sites that contain pornography, juicy Hollywood gossip, and unusual beliefs, such as that the world is flat. These are simply unprofessional. Also avoid guns and ammo sites or you might be segregated in the workplace or asked to work from home. If it is too difficult to remember your assumed profile, then recall your browsing history and try to be consistent. Each day, try to select something that shows you in the best professional image. You don't need to read the articles or books and you don't need to buy anything. The tracker simply wants to see your preferences.

In the workplace, there are people who try to enhance their status by taking credit for another person's work or by constantly promoting their accomplishments, regardless of who is listening. If work is being done on several tasks in common, make sure that any task assigned directly to you is completed first. It will be more difficult to ascertain where the problem is when several people are required to collaborate to complete a task.

AI image analysis will also use facial expression technology to augment personal profiles. The first way to fool AI image analysis is to smile a lot, even if you are not happy. Smiling reflects positivity, and a fake smile will still fool an AI tool. Deceiving the facial expression analysis tools will be difficult, although faces that lack expression are more difficult to classify. It will also be important to limit hand gestures when speaking, in case the analysis tools incorporate that movement into the data. When meeting people for the first time, it will be important to be friendly so that they have a good impression of you and so that AI will think you have good interpersonal skills. Perhaps you should tell a joke and make them laugh.

COMMUNICATION AND BROWSING

When communicating, the language content must be benign rather than emotional in case the sentiment analysis tool mistakes personal expressions to mean something bad. Refrain from sending personal emails or texts from a workplace email address. If possible, log in with a different account to send personal messages. This also applies to social media, as organizations have become increasingly interested in monitoring employees on social media websites. One possibility is to have two accounts. One account will be a profile that shows you very favorably: beautiful photo, sensible blogs, relevant likes, and connected to the most impressive people in your field. Meanwhile, you have a second account that you can use to perform all your regular interactions and not worry about being traced because it does not appear to be attached to you as an employee. Use one account to purchase normal products and click on ads for everyday products, and use a different account to hide any bad habits.

If you must surf the internet for personal use while at work, then use a private browsing feature on your browser or use your personal smartphone. A private browser prevents web browsers from recording your history. The intent is to prevent cookies from capturing data about you and building a profile in the way that normal browsers do to find something to sell you or, at the very least, something for you to click on. A more secure option is to use software that allows you to browse anonymously, such as Tor. Once configured, third-party trackers are unable to follow you and cookies are deleted when the browsing session ends. This type of solution takes you to a separate network where monitoring is not possible and traffic is encrypted. Another item to consider is to encrypt any personal files that you store on a work computer. There are several software programs that make this possible. Another strategy is to mistype important words or to use symbols, such as emojis, to represent words and to avoid being concise and clear in written or verbal communication. Also, think about using as many neutral words as possible when you communicate. This is the opposite of good business communication practice and might become a problem for your project manager or project sponsor. However, the objective is to fool or trick the machine learning algorithm in a way that it is unable to find any negative traits in your personality and cannot determine any negative sentiment that might reflect on your performance.

One expression that NLP has difficulty understanding is sarcasm. You can say anything with positive words, but when you put the emphasis at a certain place in a sentence, it changes the meaning. This is a great way to confuse AI tools. You can say, "This is a great project," and NLP thinks it is positive. Now say it again, emphasizing the first word, *this*, and turn the sentence into a question. It means something not very positive, and NLP will have trouble understanding the true meaning, although at some point in the future this may change. There are a few more suggestions that may or may not work, depending on the quality of the NLP analysis and the database used to train it. For example, using slang might fool an AI tool. Using another language or mixing words from two languages in a communication might be effective. Finally, NLP might not be aware of certain expressions that are disparaging, such as this project is "in the gutter," or this project work is "brutal and really sucks."

THE PMO AS CHANGE MANAGER

From a PMO perspective, the implications are obvious. There must be a compromise or accommodation on how AI collects data and how it is applied to all stakeholders for a project. This policy should be communicated to all stakeholders, and there needs to be an organizational commitment to compliance. If people believe that they are giving up too much personal information with only negative return, then stakeholder sentiment will go down. Even more concerning is that it may not be evident if these people learn how to deceive the sentiment analysis tools.

There are organizations that offer the ability to analyze employees on an emotional level, which presumably helps determine the best communication approach to motivate, persuade, or console them. They offer what is called cultural insights that can be used to develop a high-performance team. It also claims to reveal the unconscious, which is a bit scary but is certainly a great marketing tactic. They attempt to develop psychological profiles that allow employers to know the strengths and weaknesses of each employee. A company known as Affectiva grew from an academic background into an organization that uses deep learning to determine emotions and cognitive states (i.e., feelings), among other claims.[34] I apologize to the firms if I misrepresent their core offerings. It should be noted that these tools can be used for incredible perceptions that lead to beneficial outcomes as well as to determinations that help organizations improve the bottom line by optimizing the potential of humans to perform tasks. Psychological analysis has always been a slippery slope to navigate in a workforce, and there will be people who prefer to shield themselves from the repercussions, both positive and negative.

Do we want an organization to know our psychological profiles better than we know ourselves? People are not naturally born as experts in understanding our personal traits and the implications of our behavior. Now AI tools can not only understand us but also manipulate us into delivering the organization's goals. It is an anti-utopian environment that has the ability to sow seeds of discontent and to promote an aversion to openness. There may be a personal tipping point that occurs as an organization motivates an employee to achieve their peak performance. At some point along the way, actions taken based on AI analysis might make employees cynical about whether or not AI is providing them with any personal benefits. That point must be managed carefully by the PMO as highly sensitive and serious ethical considerations that must be navigated.

SUMMARY

Will AI tools be used to drive the organization's project objectives to a successful conclusion at the cost of human fragility? The PMO has an incredibly sensitive and difficult role to play in this area and it cannot be understated. There are short-term benefits that may outweigh

---

34 Gabi Zijderveld, "Our Evolution from Emotion AI to Human Perception AI," Affectiva, April 2, 2019, https://blog.affectiva.com/our-revolution-from-emotion-ai-to-human-perception-ai.

longer-term objectives and these may be gained at the cost of human psychological well-being. The balance is one where the PMO may be the only group that has a true vision of the cost and consequences.

CHAPTER 9
Sell the Solution

We deserve a project methodology that delivers the project scope, on schedule, and within budget for every project.

It is not enough to believe that AI tools are the answer to increased project success rates and bottom-line improvements. The PMO must convince the decision makers in the organization that it is the correct strategy. Many surveys report that executives believe that AI will change their organization, but the surveys fail to reveal how they expect adoption will actually happen. The PMO is in a unique position to influence the direction of project-based organizations. They have access to executives who fund procurement decisions and can establish pilot projects that will prove the value of AI tools. The PMO also has access to project team members who might see themselves as victims of AI adoption, and the PMO can convince these employees that the value of using AI to change project processes outweighs any reasonable concerns. The goal, after all, is to participate in a successful project and to be recognized for contributing to project success. The PMO should be the owner of the standard project process used by all projects, and they can connect all the elements that will make AI tools work.

DRIVE THE CHANGE IN METHODOLOGY

Convincing executives, employees, and project managers is an exercise in change management. There must be honest communication, adequate training, and an analysis and description of how the adoption of AI tools will change the roles of everyone. Convincing executives to acquire AI tools is probably the easiest part because they're already aware of AI tools being deployed in other organizations. The increase in project success rates and the reduced cost of implementing projects can be detailed clearly enough to warrant the introduction and use of AI tools. The cost tends to be low and the payback is fast if the appropriate AI tools are introduced in the correct part of the process. The issue, as always, will be the availability of data to allow the tools to function properly. The importance of data can be clearly stated but is often given insufficient attention.

For project team members, using AI tools will have a low impact because the majority of their work remains on completing specific project tasks. The biggest issue is the potential invasion of privacy or the unfettered distribution of their personal information. This requires the PMO to work closely with the organization, and especially the IT group, to ensure the security of personal information. There must be a balance between divulging personal information and the amount of data needed to train AI models. There are situations where giving an AI tool our personal information is beneficial, as is evident when communicating with chatbots. For example, people like to be addressed by their names, even when they are communicating with a machine.

Convincing project managers that adopting AI tools is a good strategy might be more difficult than it would seem. Certainly, project managers prefer to be recognized with successful projects than with unsuccessful ones. However, most of the changes to the project methodology require change to the way that a project manager performs work and makes decisions. Project managers gain authority and credibility by making decisions, which also provides them with the opportunity to exhibit leadership. With AI tools, project managers lose some of the decision-making ability because the AI tool retains and analyzes far more data than a human brain. That does not make AI intimidating, but it may appear to degrade the value of a project manager's role because AI tools can lead to less responsibility for a project manager and less work. Some project managers might believe that the objective of deploying AI tools is to eliminate the project manager's role. This is debated elsewhere in this book, and the attitude of a project manager will contribute to the decision. The project manager's role will change to include the interpretation of AI output as well as the management of project data. The project manager will be the person who utilizes AI tools and validates the results before taking the project in the next direction based on AI output. The project manager will become the translator of the results, which is a valuable responsibility. In fact, if the PMO can convince the project manager of the value of AI, then the project manager can become the change agent who convinces all stakeholders of the importance of implementing AI tools throughout the project process to achieve the organization's goals.

The strategy for AI implementation in project management must include the ability to take advantage of other technologies, such as data mining and the Internet of Things (IoT). Data mining should be the first step in the assessment of the project methodology. Given sufficient data, a data mining exercise can determine why projects that succeed are successful and identify the reasons why projects have failed. This can form the basis for initiating a change to the project methodology. However, to be successful, the process must be continuous and not a one-time event.

For IoT, the pervasiveness of sensors is only the beginning. Cameras capture progress on a construction project. A web scraper takes a snapshot of progress on software deployment. A dash cam tracks and records deliveries. The myriad of IoT devices that will eventually be deployed for projects will provide an enormous amount of data. This can be vital for a PMO that needs to track multiple projects as close to real time as possible. In addition to determining an IoT strategy of sensor deployment, there must be a strategy for how to manage and store the data, unless the plan is to train a model with streaming data and not retain any. Perhaps IoT data will be directly fed as updates to the project schedule. The data collected might also be used as part of managing the project team. In this case, the issues of security, privacy, and confidentiality all must be considered and resolved.

SELL THE SOLUTION

The first step in making a change is to develop a clear and compelling value statement that the organization approves. This will be unique to each organization and aligned with its strategy and mission. The PMO must clearly explain how AI tools for project management are an essential element for ongoing success. AI tools can reduce costs and accelerate the achievement of goals. For project management, there will be an increasing number of projects that include deploying AI into an organization. It is incredulous to think that these projects can be successful when the current project methodology does not rely on any AI tools to manage the project.

The next step in change management is communication, so the organization must communicate the strategy, assuming it has one, for how AI tools will be introduced. Will there be a pilot project, or will a single tool be implemented across multiple projects? How and when will the results be available? What is the next step? A strategy or roadmap is useful to inform all stakeholders and to foster communication about the process changes and timeline. Checkpoints can be included along the way. Evaluations will be performed and, based on results to date, a decision will be made on how to proceed. Communicating the importance of data is crucial and will lead to a greater understanding of how AI tools work.

Training is also a major component of change management. AI has become a buzzword, with some degree of mystery, so training must get into the details of exactly how machine learning and NLP tools really work to make projects more successful. Machine learning is not an easy concept to understand; therefore, explaining the basic concepts and how they have an impact on the project methodology is important.

Process redesign is another component of change management, and this will be the crucial part. It is always nice to have employees involved, but in this situation, the PMO is in the best position to provide a vision of how AI tools will work. The process must be disrupted by AI tools, and this type of change is not easy for many people to accept. The PMO needs to create and communicate the strategy for how the project methodology will change and the timeline proposed for implementing the changes. The objective is to communicate the positive results that can be obtained by using AI tools and the benefit to the whole organization.

IMPLEMENTATION STRATEGY

Now that the overwhelming possibilities of AI for project management are evident, the question is where or how to start. My suggestion is that because data is a critical element, it is the best place to begin. Performing data mining on the existing project data can reveal interesting insights. Is there a parameter that is set in the planning stage and is always changed after the project starts? This might be a scope item, a milestone date, or a risk. The next step is to use data mining to identify the set of conditions that is present when that change occurs. This is a way to slowly build your knowledge about the project data while gaining unexpected insights. It also forces you to think about structured data for projects. Perhaps the project data has structured data fields, and if not, then a software program using NLP can pull key information into a structured format that can then be analyzed.

Once the data availability is resolved, a pilot project can begin with a focus to solve a specific problem. A vendor tool can be acquired or an internal machine learning tool can be developed. This must be part of an overall strategy and it must fit into a holistic perspective of managing projects. It helps to think of this process as building a set of tools and not individual solutions. There also needs to be alignment in solving the organization's problems with a more holistic approach of making projects better as well as determining the best AI tools for an organization.

In addition, the PMO must identify and manage any restrictions that are defined by the organization. In some cases, data security policy will restrict internal data so that it is not allowed to go to another site or another country or to be viewed by an unauthorized person. For example, it can be unacceptable to store data in a cloud where the backup location is not advertised and is possibly in a foreign country. As technology changes, cloud storage companies are rapidly developing new methods to ensure data security. Having an external developer create tools to be used at the organization's site can be accomplished in two ways. First, machine learning tools that use but do not retain any of the data can be created. Next, developing a tool to be used by an organization without having sample data is difficult. However, it is possible for a developer to simulate the data and build the algorithm using synthetic (i.e., fake) data that resembles the true structured data and then bring it on-site to test the algorithm with real data.

Technology rarely works consistently well and does not work at all unless it has the proper data. To achieve the bottom-line improvements, someone has to oversee the process, update the data, and ensure that the AI tools are performing the way they need to perform. Buying an AI tool is not like buying a desk. AI is a software program, or more likely a series of software programs, that interact with each other. They need maintenance to continue to produce results. The PMO is in the best position to evaluate, implement, and identify the value of AI tools across the project management processes and on an ongoing basis. They can also address any outliers or events that do not fit into the normal model of a machine learning algorithm. The PMO becomes the caretaker of project success. The ongoing need for project managers will be determined by the success of AI tools. As productivity increases, the organization can decide to reduce the number of project managers or let them add more value to the process in other ways. Project managers will be vital for process feedback and adjustments as well as for managing project data issues.

A new responsibility for the PMO can be the creation of an AI safety role. As AI advances rapidly, the machine learning algorithms must stay consistent and in control.[35] This is not about becoming sentient but about being able to manage outcomes of poorly created models. The example used by Nick Bostrom in his book *Superintelligence* is about using a machine learning algorithm to optimize the production of paperclips.[36] The AI tool has a clear objective to produce paperclips. To increase efficiency, the machine learning tool optimizes production in a way that produces negative results in another area. For example, it takes over the capacity of the equipment used to produce staplers, which results in staplers not achieving their production objectives. In project management, the AI tools being used on a project should not be able to create a negative impact on other projects, the environment, or the resources. There might be projects in the past where, in order to optimize the result, the project created a detrimental effect on the environment. Perhaps it created more pollution or it removed trees unnecessarily to make the project more efficient.

Similarly, human resources should be protected in case the machine learning algorithm determines that working a twenty-hour day on a task is more efficient. AI tools have objectives but they also need boundaries. The PMO can determine the boundaries that are the best fit for the organization as well as for the external environment. The concept of AI safety is fairly new, and investigation must be performed regarding what other organizations have in place. Collaboration with AI researchers and AI tool builders can help this effort. To summarize, we must create a project with the objective of changing how we implement projects.

---

35   James Guszcza, Iyad Rahwan, Will Bible, Manuel Cebrian, and Vic Katyal, "Why We Need to Audit Algorithms," *Harvard Business Review*, November 28, 2018, https://hbr.org/2018/11/why-we-need-to-audit-algorithms.
36   Nick Bostrom, *Superintelligence: Paths, Dangers, Strategies* (New York: Oxford University Press, 2016).

THE PITFALLS

Implementing any new technology has problems that need to be understood and managed properly. In 2019, IBM Watson came under increasing criticism for failing to deliver positive results in a project to deliver treatment recommendations for oncology patients. In some cases, the treatment suggested was unsafe and incorrect.[37] Among the many reasons for the lack of success is the inability of NLP to understand medical texts and interpret the meaning in the way that a doctor would. This is a lesson for the PMO because project management also has unique jargon and complicated concepts, such as critical path analysis. Fortunately, project concepts are not updated as frequently as the release of new pharmaceutical products.

Implementing new technology can result in many problems for both large and small organizations, and the PMO must have a clear strategy in place. There is any number of ways to fail, and large organizations are capable of making large mistakes. Similarly, smaller organizations can fail by not having knowledgeable resources and, especially, an insufficient amount of retained historical data. AI in some ways is simply another technology, and the PMO must understand how it works in order to create a good strategy and successful implementation. It is also likely that other technologies will be considered at the same time. The PMO needs to ensure that the creation of a comprehensive strategy for digital transformation does not bog down and delay the implementation of machine learning tools. AI requires a different way of thinking about how to use software, and different IT resources are needed if the algorithms are being created internally.

---

37   Eliza Strickland, "How IBM Watson Overpromised and Underdelivered on AI Health Care," IEEE Spectrum, April 2, 2019, https://spectrum.ieee.org/biomedical/diagnostics/how-ibm-watson-overpromised-and-underlivered-on-ai-health-care.

The list of potential pitfalls is rather large. Here are some of them:

- Lack of knowledge on how to use machine learning results

- Tools are too narrowly focused and lack a holistic approach

- Insufficient data that results in underfitting and inaccurate results

- Algorithms that are improperly created, resulting in incorrect interpretation

- The wrong AI tool is selected for the situation or available data

- An AI tool is implemented but there is poor communication around the usage and results

OVERCOMING AI RESISTANCE

One of the main challenges that a PMO faces is resistance to change, especially when dealing with a supposedly frightening technology such as AI. Will AI reduce or eliminate jobs? Possibly, although it depends on how the organization manages the change. If AI tools are not implemented properly, who is responsible? The owner of the AI tool or whoever is providing funding will be responsible. Will AI implementation create unforeseen problems in the organization? Probably, and this is why the PMO needs a good change management strategy. There are numerous fears, and the PMO can start managing them with information and training.

The greatest ally for implementing AI seems to be executives, as surveys continue to show that executives believe they need AI solutions to remain competitive.[38] The PMO is in a perfect position to bridge the gap between executives who want AI for the competitive advantage and lower-level employees who are wondering about the consequences of AI, mainly due to misconceptions and the potential for job loss. Once the PMO acquires an understanding of how AI works for project management, they can communicate this effectively and alleviate some of the organizational anxiety. The PMO can highlight changes that will address current issues and make the organization stronger. The employees who participate in AI deployment will become more knowledgeable and gain valuable experience for their careers. Effective communication and good facilitation skills are needed for the PMO to be successful in managing the change.

Because AI tools create privacy and data security issues for employees, the PMO must work with the organization to review policies and procedures to identify any necessary adjustments. The PMO may also want to verify the effectiveness of the current policies in place. The main way to overcome resistance is to provide facts. AI tools, similar to other new technologies, provide increased value as long as they are implemented and used properly.

SUMMARY

The PMO is in a pivotal position, with the ability to convince senior executives that AI tools can change the project methodology to accelerate the accomplishment of the organization's objectives. Roles will change, but there is a willingness and perhaps an eagerness to take advantage of the technology. The PMO must identify the value and communicate it in a clear and compelling way. As the most knowledgeable entity in project processes and problems, the PMO can determine

---

38 Vanian, "Most Executives Fear Their Companies Will Fail if They Don't Adopt A.I."

how AI tools fit into a redesigned process. Implementation requires a thoughtful strategy that aligns with the organization's willingness to make improvements. Successful implementation of AI tools brings more knowledge and starts a positive cycle of process improvement. This is a large challenge, and the PMO is an ideal group to make it happen. Implementation is not a one-time event, and the next chapter discusses the change in roles due to ongoing AI implementation. It is important to build a successful process for implementing the tools because this technology continues to develop amazing capability, and we need to apply that to how we manage projects.

CHAPTER 10
Changing Roles

We are at the cusp of a revolution in project methods, and all project stakeholders need to embrace the change.

The PMO must think about the following three phases of strategy that have an impact on the role of the project manager. During the first phase, the project manager needs to be the person who manages data, accepts and uses the new technology, and provides feedback to improve the tools. For the second phase, there will be a more significant influx of AI tools. The project manager must collaborate with the machine learning tools and implement the project methodology changes that provide bottom-line improvement for the organization. At this stage, the need for a project manager is reduced but not eliminated, and a single project manager will be able to handle a larger number of projects. The third phase occurs when a self-driving project starts to take over, and a project manager will oversee any project anomalies. There are no timelines for the three phases, and they are likely to depend on both the organization and the availability of AI tools for project management. However, the AI capability for the first phase exists now.

In many industries, human tasks are being replaced by AI or other software tools. It should be expected that more project tasks will be achieved either by automated tools or at least by a smaller project team that uses AI to complete their tasks. AI is also expected to result in higher-quality work that has fewer errors. Software tools will be able to collect information from a variety of databases and review documents regarding project management concepts to create a standard or even best practice process. Some of the project teams of the future will consist of both humans and software-based team members. Dashboards will be driven by AI tools that scour the project data and deliver updates or results as needed. A review of the changing roles includes the project manager, the project team, and the PMO.

A NEW ROLE FOR PROJECT MANAGERS

If the self-driving project is the final phase of project changes, then emphasis needs to be placed on how that will impact the project manager role. For a project manager, time-consuming tasks, such as document preparation, communication, and problem-solving that involves project-based logic, will decline. For any project, there are numerous documents to prepare, and the size, amount, and complexity will be determined by the project or organizational requirements. The best current approach is to use a template from a previous similar project so that customer requirements are translated into a project scope and work breakdown structure. This builds the baselines for budget and schedule. When an AI tool uses NLP to create documents, this must be based on a large repository of historical project information. Because the definition of a project is that each one is unique, the project manager must include the new requirements that make this project different. A more valuable use of AI tools is to have NLP scan the completed documents to capture errors or omissions. Some of these tools already exist and are available now. The role of the project manager is to oversee the successful use of AI tools, which includes finding greater efficiency in preparing the documents as well as ensuring their accuracy.

A project manager recently told me that her organization has "flaky" budgets because they were prepared from flaky scope statements. Some organizations don't have the time or the resources to do this properly, and other organizations simply want to move to the execution stage as quickly as possible so that they can show progress. With a project that has an external client, it is likely that project managers will be needed so that they can help understand and successfully complete the client requirements. This is an important step in creating a viable project and one that is based on accurate requirements. There were many times when, in my experience, the client specification and what the client actually wanted were not the same, and it was only through face-to-face dialogue that this became evident.

Communication is a task that many people believe can be performed only by a project manager, but self-directed teams can use tools such as Slack to communicate effectively. The project manager mainly communicates changes to the project work while motivating, persuading, or directing team members. In the first phase of deploying AI tools for project management, these tasks are not likely to be eliminated, although there are AI tools that can significantly reduce the amount of communication required by a project manager. For example, if the scope statement is sufficiently defined and there are few, if any, scope changes, then this translates into a reduced amount of churn in project activities and will decrease the amount of information that needs to be updated and communicated to the project team. Similarly, if the risk plan is comprehensive, is clearly defined, and has adequate risk responses due to analysis by an AI tool, then that should reduce the amount of project work and subsequent communication. In terms of project performance, tools already exist that provide feedback to workers on task completion and the timeliness or inadequacy of completing project activities. In terms of communicating with external parties, there will be less human contact. For example, in the retail industry, it was estimated that in 2020, 85 percent of all customer interactions will be managed by chatbots.[39]

Using project management knowledge to solve difficult project problems is one of the most important tasks for a project manager. Sometimes there is only one solution to a problem, such as adding more resources. However, a task like performing project crashing requires the ability to understand the critical path and how to manipulate it to find the best solution at the lowest negative impact. In some situations, a project manager may use simulation software to evaluate

---

39 Heather Pemberton Levy, "Gartner Predicts a World of Exponential Change," Smarter with Gartner, October 18, 2016, https://www.gartner.com/smarterwithgartner/gartner-predicts-a-virtual-world-of-exponential-change.

several possible solutions for a problem. An AI tool performs this by assessing all the data, selecting the highest probability solution, and ensuring a holistic solution that considers all aspects of the project. This is a complex model to create, and if it is in place, the project manager needs only to verify the solution and make the proper changes. The result is less time spent analyzing each option, including all the extenuating factors.

Many project managers spend time speaking with members of the project team or the customer to make sure that they have the latest information. This might be helpful in understanding why a problem occurs, uncovering new information, and allowing a project team member to voice an opinion. This is a way to gather information that might not otherwise be available or that might be slightly inaccurate if not communicated directly from the source. Information gathering is exactly what is needed for AI tools. It cannot be haphazard and must be structured and consistent. One challenge for gathering data for AI tools is to make sure that all relevant information is collected and available in a structured and timely way. Opinions and thoughts must be separated from facts unless the opinions collectively indicate an issue that can be managed using sentiment analysis. With AI tools, the project manager can spend less time wandering aimlessly and more time collecting real-time data. Another task of a project manager or staff in the PMO is to negotiate with various people or groups, especially when resources are required. A project manager can be valuable if they know the basics of negotiating, but for difficult scenarios, it has always been a good practice to use an expert negotiator. As indicated in the section on the self-driving project, the project manager's role will change to collaborating with AI tools, and in the process, learn how to negotiate a better result.

The world of project management is not without controversy. One of the more common topics is whether or not the project manager needs to be a technical expert. For a construction project, the project manager should have some knowledge of construction. For a software deployment, the project manager should have some IT background. One school of thought says that a well-trained project management expert who has completed numerous projects does not need to have a technical background. After all, the subject matter expert can either be part of the project team or a person who the project manager can contact for expert advice. On the other hand, it is argued that the lack of technical knowledge by a project manager leads to the inability to make proper and timely decisions. In this situation, the project manager is blind to certain nuances or threats that can derail a project and lead to significant problems, such as schedule delays, substantial overspending, and poor quality. As a consequence, some organizations hire a technical expert to lead a project, then attempt to provide project management training. This has mixed results. There are times when the technical project manager makes quick decisions without consulting experts who would have provided input for a better decision. There are also times when the lack of project management knowledge leaves the technical project manager unable to foresee problems or take a greater perspective that includes all aspects of managing a project. They may be a technical expert in a specific field, but they are not an expert in managing all the moving pieces of a project.

Regardless of whether it is a good plan, more organizations will view AI tools as a mechanism to reduce the requirement for actual project management skills and to simply have technical or functional experts perform the project management role. This is already happening without AI tools, but AI tools will accelerate this shift. One organization that I worked with had a professional services group of skilled project managers who helped guide the technical experts in deploying software at a client's site. They tracked the completion of tasks, managed risks, resolved issues, and provided communication to all stakeholders. A new CEO joined the organization and laid off all the project managers, believing that the technical experts could easily perform the project management role in addition to their existing technical responsibilities once they received a little more training. This philosophy will only increase as AI tools are adopted by organizations, but the success of this approach is unpredictable. However, AI tools have the capability to supply both technical skills and project management knowledge. A better approach than eliminating trained project managers is to develop a strategy that complements organizational decisions.

Project managers continually need different or enhanced skills, something that seems to be an ongoing topic. With AI tools, one of the most important capabilities is the willingness to accept and work with new technology. There can be no fear, arrogance, or stubbornness. Project managers who blame AI for every failure are probably not going to last very long. They need to find ways to make the AI-infused process work. The project manager also must find a way to leverage AI so that projects are more successful and less costly to implement. Another new skill required by project managers to utilize AI is data literacy. This is especially important at the early stage of AI tool deployment into project management processes. Is there sufficient structured data for machine learning tools to be effective? If not, can NLP be used to capture and extract the data from project documents that is needed to make the proper classification and prediction analysis? New skills must include AI interpretation at a basic level, which means a better understanding of mathematics, especially statistical methods.

It may no longer be necessary to seek a project manager who is a great communicator when AI tools take over most of this responsibility, as 64 percent of people in one survey responded that they would trust a robot more than their current manager when requesting advice.[40] The new role of a project manager is to focus on the project

---

40 Celina Bertallee, "New Study: 64% of People Trust a Robot More Than Their Manager," Oracle, October 15, 2019, https://www.oracle.com/corporate/pressrelease/robots-at-work-101519.html.

methodology and how to increase the value of AI tools that are implemented. Project managers can also initiate studies for new areas where AI tools should be used. One final observation is how project managers can use AI results in their favor when working in a dysfunctional organization or on a dysfunctional project. For example, the project manager takes responsibility for a project and uses the AI predictor tool to discover that the project has only a 52 percent probability of success. In spite of this result, the organization decides that the project must be executed, regardless of the poor or incomplete planning. The project manager is given instructions to proceed with the project, but the project fails in typical fashion, late to schedule and significantly overspent. When the project manager's performance review highlights this failure as a below-expectation outcome, the project manager now has proof that the project was already likely to fail, in spite of the efforts to complete it successfully. AI tools can expose poor management and bad decisions.

CAN THE PROJECT MANAGER BE REPLACED?

Will AI eventually replace the project manager as outlined in the self-driving project? Many people, especially project managers, believe that replacing a project manager with AI is not possible. What is it that a project manager does that an AI-based tool cannot perform better? AI has greater memory, performs more accurate analysis, and makes faster decisions. Certainly, an AI project manager would have more business acumen than any of us. The most common argument is that an AI tool cannot perform effective people management, and this is where I disagree. Think of the worst manager you ever had. The one with anger issues, who took credit for all your good ideas, never recognized or commented on anything that you did well, was extremely self-interested, played political games, and gave you a bad performance review based on personal bias and not on actual outcomes. Is this the project manager you want to work for? There is no guarantee that any project manager will be the model of leadership that is often expected. Project managers are people and they have flaws. Many of them are terrible at managing people. This is the first reason why organizations will be tempted to try to manage projects without a project manager. In fact, a recent survey revealed that 30 percent of employees would be willing to replace their current manager with a robot. The fascinating results identified several reasons why employees would agree to this, including that they disliked their boss and they felt that their boss was biased, incompetent, and lacked empathy.[41]

Computer-based tools that give instant feedback on performance already exist. A simple example is the Kahoot! app that I use in my classroom. Students receive instant feedback regarding how well they perform, and another feature allows them to compare their knowledge to others in the same group. AI tools have the ability to recognize facial expressions, something that many managers cannot do effectively. Managers may make rude or insensitive comments, oblivious to the personal impact. An AI-based project manager may not take you out for lunch or discuss the latest viral video of a cat. On the other hand, an AI project manager won't harass you or find a way to refuse a promotion because of your race, gender, religion, or other personal bias. Rewards and recognition will be based on a more objective perspective of performance, skills, and accomplishments.

---

41 Kevin Kruse, "30% of Workers Would Replace Their Boss with a Robot," *Forbes*, September 18, 2019, https://www.forbes.com/sites/kevinkruse/2019/09/18/30-of-workers-would-replace-their-boss-with-a-robot/#28c4ed017eeb.

COLLABORATING WITH AI TOOLS

This chapter began with a more realistic look at a day in the life of a future project manager who collaborates with AI tools. While the self-driving project might be anywhere from five to twelve years away, the following scenario is possible within the next two years. This, of course, depends on how aggressive an organization is with AI deployment for project management. The tools described next exist now but have not been customized for projects or deployed directly into project processes.

A typical day starts with arriving at an office or working from a home-based office. The project manager asks a virtual assistant for a project status, along with any anomalies that need to be addressed immediately. Anomalies are incidents, decisions, or results that have the potential to cause project problems, such as schedule delays, overspending, or achieving scope. The project manager requests that the AI tool identify the best method to resolve any of these issues, and the AI tool presents a solution that includes a probability of success. Next, the project manager asks for a summary of the project, which includes an evaluation of the budget, schedule, risks, and any other items that are deemed important to the project. This information gives the project manager a benchmark for current project activities. Change requests are reviewed and, when they are approved, an assessment is made for how they can be implemented effectively without a negative impact on the project baselines.

Based on this status report, the project manager now asks for a projection of project completion and any issues that might create a variance to the project baselines for the duration of the project. The project manager addresses and resolves any issues that the AI tools are unable to manage themselves, which typically means that they did not find enough data to provide a statistically significant answer. In this case, the project manager makes a note that more structured data is required for this area of the project. The next item the project manager addresses is communication, which starts with project stakeholders. An AI tool has already assessed the key psychological factors and personality traits for all team members, and the project manager uses this to respond to any concerns as well as to properly motivate each person on the project team. For other stakeholders, the project manager reviews the stakeholder communication plan and searches for any recent utterances in terms of verbal or written content about the project. These are classified as positive, negative, or neutral. For negative sentiment, the project manager uses an AI tool to assess how to effectively communicate with the specific stakeholder to discover what response will give the most positive result.

As the day progresses, the project manager speaks to each project team member, remembering to use words, phrases, and sentences in a manner that is customized to each person so that they understand the communication. The project manager checks whether the client or project sponsor has any concerns regarding the project. As usual, an event occurs that threatens the project, perhaps a new risk is identified or an employee quits. The project manager uses AI tools to find the best response and takes steps to update the project data that feeds the machine learning algorithms so that more accurate models are created. The new risk should have been identified before the project began. In addition, the probability of the employee leaving should have been considered in the resource assignment and added to the risk register. If the crisis event cannot be averted, the project manager looks for a creative solution, perhaps something outside the project environment. This might be a vendor solution or finding a new resource for the one who left. If this increases the cost, then an AI tool will suggest project efficiencies that can recover the increased cost at the least disturbance to the project baselines. The project manager also might use an AI tool to look for a creative solution. Although many solutions may be thought of as creative, it is likely that a usable solution has been implemented previously, perhaps in another organization or with a similar type of project. The AI tool is a replacement for a subject matter expert and is maintained by the PMO, as it is typically used across a portfolio and not only for a specific project.

In addition to reviewing progress on the project, the project manager spends a significant amount of time ensuring that project data is captured, structured properly, and stored for use by machine learning algorithms. This updating process is important for accurate algorithm results. The next scenario is an event that is escalated to the project manager by the project team. The customer wants to make a change to the scope of the project without raising a change request and without providing additional project funding. The first problem with this scenario is that the AI tools at the start of the project should have detected that this type of change had a high probability of occurring and added it to the risk register. Next, with a complete psychological analysis, the AI tools should predict with a high probability that this particular customer is likely to engage in this type of behavior where the scope statement is approved but the customer wants more functionality before the project is complete. In reality, this is a common occurrence when projects are going well and customers see more potential benefits from the new project. Scope creep is often due to excitement and not an inadequate scope statement. Fortunately, in this situation the project manager negotiated a contingency reserve, and, regardless of the outcome, the project manager is able to maintain the project budget and schedule to deliver a successful result.

The later part of the day is spent communicating with other departments, such as the IT group, to make sure that the most recent project data is appropriately structured and available for the machine learning algorithms. A significant change to the role of the project manager is that acquiring and storing data is now one of their priorities. Project management decision-making will be aided by AI tools, and the project manager is the person who communicates the results rather than makes the decisions. Exceptions are rare, and when they occur, the project manager must find a way to incorporate this new data into the AI tools and to use the tools to investigate and determine a solution. Finally, the project manager attends a meeting with the PMO to discuss the next project and how to negotiate with the new customer. It will be important to have a complete scope statement and to present a clear and achievable schedule and budget. The PMO ensures that the project manager has taken all the steps to capture and report project data so that it may be used by machine learning tools across all projects. The change in responsibilities is shown in table 6.

Table 6: Example of Changing Responsibilities

Activity	Current Responsibility	Future Responsibility
Data acquisition and maintenance	IT	PMO/project manager
Decision-making	Project manager	AI tools
Managing outliers	Project manager	PMO/project manager
Maintain/update AI tools		PMO/IT
Communication: messaging	Project manager	AI tools/project manager
Stakeholder communication	Project manager	AI tools/project manager

The result is that a single project manager is now able to manage several projects at once because each project takes less time. This is a significant bottom-line savings for the organization because each project now costs less to implement. There are also fewer exceptions, changes, or crisis events that disrupt the project process and create additional work beyond the project environment.

A NEW ROLE FOR THE PROJECT TEAM

The project team also has to learn to work with AI tools, although they probably have much less direct interaction. Workflow tools that already use AI in the background will be enhanced and continue to be used. The project team members are likely to receive direction in more or less the usual way that communication occurs in the project. Because there is increased importance placed on data management, the team members must diligently ensure that structured data is captured and stored. Any data outliers or unusual events need to be well documented, including the set of conditions that were present when they occurred.

A significant bottom-line savings is the possibility of replacing project team members with AI tools. In fact, this idea might seem easier to accomplish than replacing a project manager. In some globally dispersed teams, the project manager has little interaction with a team member who performs the work. Is it acceptable to replace a team member if an AI tool can produce the same results? A review of this must include several considerations that might be important to a project manager who is responsible for completing the project successfully. Specifically, these concerns include skills, communication, personal interaction, and handling change.

Project team member skills tend to be specific or technical, based on their education, experience, and training. In addition, they need the ability to understand and promote the organization's goals in how they interpret and complete work that is not clearly defined. AI tools should be able to incorporate the education, experience, and training requirements equal to or better than a team member. The question is if the AI tool can adequately reflect the nuances of an organization's mission and objectives. Note that at this point it is assumed that the team member is actually knowledgeable, willing, and capable of incorporating an organization's sense of direction. Some employees may be unaware or simply not care because the culture of the organization is not sufficiently supportive.

While AI is known for automating more simple tasks, it has a cognitive ability that can now perform more complex functions. AI tools can detect configuration errors and perform software tests that were previously performed only by IT professionals.[42] The following is an example to help understand the possibilities of AI performing project team tasks. For a customer relationship management (CRM) software deployment, there is normally a subject matter expert who becomes part of the project team for implementation. The subject matter expert performs a functional role that registers clients for the organization's services. The goal is to change this to a self-service model where the clients register themselves and submit their own profiles. The subject matter expert—or functional prime, as they are sometimes called—has knowledge of how the current process is performed and knows a myriad of current and past problems that must be avoided in the new system implementation. The team therefore includes a functional representative and an IT person who specializes in CRM configuration. With AI, neither of these are needed on the project team. The functional representative is the expert on how the organization's business process works, such as the process for registering new members. The functional representative writes the process or explains the process verbally to the AI tool that uses NLP to collect all the data. The AI tool also asks questions about every aspect of the process, especially to uncover anomalies. These anomalies can then be classified and either included or discarded as not worth continuing in the new process.

Once the AI tool understands the process, it decides on the best configuration for the CRM tool for that process. This is no longer a "custom" solution but a blend of what is required by the organization and what is most efficient for this type of deployment. This reduces or eliminates two roles in the project: the functional expert and the

---

42 "Artificial Intelligence for Faster and Smarter UI Testing," SmartBear.com, accessed November 26, 2019, https://smartbear.com/resources/ebooks/artificial-intelligence-for-faster-and-smater-ui.

configuration person.[43] The desired outcome of the interface between these two people on a project is to create a comprehensive list of requirements, something that is rarely done and often misunderstood. An AI tool can create the comprehensive requirements list as well as provide the configuration based on the requirements. Unlike a human, the AI tool not only remembers every detail but also continues to investigate areas that are unclear or not sufficiently defined based on what has occurred in similar projects of this type.

In this scenario, the project manager is left to manage higher-level responsibilities, such as ensuring that an IT strategy for deploying the solution is in place, if a hosted solution is required, and the amount of backup, security, or other criteria required. The project manager also must ensure that employees attend the training and can properly manage the new process. Functional department employees tend to retain old habits, which may not be the most effective attitude when attempting to migrate to a new system. Another responsibility of the project manager will be overseeing the data migration. Once again, AI tools are available to help map data to specific fields, and this will be easier with an AI tool that is also in charge of the new software configuration process.

One benefit is the reduced cost of the back-and-forth dialogue between the functional prime and the configuration person. The issue has always been whether or not the configuration person truly understands the business process, which they usually do not, and the functional person is normally lost in understanding all the implications of configuration decisions. A critical area will be understanding where functional areas interact, a typical example being finance. There might be a fee when a new person performs self-registration, and this is a

---

43 Mariya Yao, "6 Ways AI Transforms How We Develop Software," *Forbes*, April 18, 2018, https://www.forbes.com/sites/mariyayao/2018/04/18/6-ways-ai-transforms-how-we-develop-software/#7490122c26cf.

task that falls under functional confirmation or in some cases requires an interface to a different system. In my experience, interfaces have always been troublesome. Each system might be upgraded separately at different times, and any upgrade might force changes to be made in the other system. This can be annoying and is probably one of the reasons why organizations moved to enterprise resource management (ERP) systems. An AI tool can decide the best process for completing an interface, although it should be a normal software program that is used to monitor each program and to identify upgrades and changes as they are required.

Work capabilities are changing for software installations, such as ERP and CRM deployments. Before the current tools existed, software programmers wrote code for each function required. With current tools, the IT specialist performs configuration, which means that the code is already written and the software is only customized to the client's requirements by identifying each setting that must be used. In the future, AI tools will predict the configuration settings based on an analysis of the organization's business processes and how to optimize them for specific objectives. For user acceptance testing, the current process is to have a few key users perform essential functions in a development environment. This is limited because it is too time consuming to perform all the tests. With AI tools, all functions can be tested because the AI tools are not limited by time. This will reduce errors and improve the schedule. These are only two examples of how AI tools will change the meaning of a project team. The PMO must manage this new environment.

Building a connection of mutual trust and respect with a team member is probably the characteristic that a project manager will miss the most in not having a human team member. There are times when a project manager has trusted allies who rise above simply completing their assigned tasks and help the project manager in numerous other areas, such as keeping in touch with team sentiment, passing on the latest organizational rumors, and providing other news that might have an impact on the project. The team member might also be a good contact who can be used to discreetly discuss strategy or review alternatives to resolving a project issue. An AI tool is certainly capable of maintaining the results of team sentiment. If there are fewer human team members, the number of rumors will also be reduced. Having access to a virtual assistant powered by an intelligent agent that is knowledgeable in project management is a good start. However, the agent needs to be able to summarize any unofficial news and to determine how valid it is and whether or not the project manager should be informed. Using a secure account, the project manager will be able to use the virtual assistant with machine learning capabilities to review alternative strategies for project issues before making a decision.

In discussing how AI tools can improve project communication and lead to higher success in projects, I invariably meet project managers who point out a project team member who has no interest in project success. They barely perform their tasks, with some playing office politics to the detriment of the project manager. What a difficult situation. We are not always able to select our team members, so it is possible that some project teams consist of people who are negative influences. It would be easy to suggest that the project manager needs more skills training in leadership and communication and especially in how to manage difficult people.

AI tools might also help, although it will not be easy. Typical suggestions include remaining calm, avoiding judgment, and continuing to show respect. This situation is obviously not specific to project management. The area where AI tools might help is with an analysis of verbal and written communication. AI can detect mental health issues or stress, and both of these might be the root cause of the person's behavior. IT tools can also be used to closely monitor the project results as tasks progress so that a project manager can be proactive and perhaps add additional resources where required before the project falls too deeply into trouble. The role of the project manager is to report results in a nonjudgmental way. For office politics, AI can assess personality types and perhaps help the project manager discover the issues or reasons for a person's behavior. There are numerous resources that suggest ways to deal with a person engaged in office politics. Honesty is one that works, but each situation is different, and perhaps insight provided by AI tools can move the effort in the right direction.

A NEW ROLE FOR THE PMO

The new PMO is responsible for deploying AI to change the project methodology and also to ensure that the changes are followed. To learn from any initial failures, vigilance is required on actual project results, especially when the goal is 100 percent success for every project. Metrics are more important at every stage of the project because trends can be monitored and become part of the data that is required by machine learning tools. The PMO also needs metrics to demonstrate the success of the new methodology and to show gains made by implementing AI processes. The PMO is responsible for auditing to ensure that AI systems conform to standard practices and meet employee and societal expectations, especially in terms of ethics and privacy. If the existence of a PMO results in a certain power structure in the organization, the power structure will become even more evident with the deployment of AI tools.

PMO staff will continue to initiate, manage, and monitor projects, but with AI they now have a new and powerful tool. AI will not only improve the project processes but also may provide surprising additional benefits.[44] Similar to the skills changes needed for project managers,

---

44   Ellen Friedman, "With Machine Learning and AI, the Win Isn't Always Where You Think," Mapr, April 30, 2019, https://mapr.com/blog/with-machine-learning-and-ai-the-win-isnt-always-where-you-think-it-is.

the PMO must become more comfortable with math and statistics, especially regression analysis. There will be a learning curve as AI tools are adopted, and increased training is required to achieve optimal results. In addition—and this should be obvious—the PMO must take control of data management for projects. This will be a significant role because 70 to 90 percent of the time spent for machine learning tool development is with managing data.[45] Having this knowledge and knowing the advantages and pitfalls of the new AI tools, the PMO needs to identify the training required for all project staff.

The biggest challenge facing a PMO is to provide value to the organization on an ongoing basis. Using AI permits numerous possibilities to demonstrate greater value. A measurable example is the ability to deliver the project successfully at a lower cost. The lower cost is achieved by using the AI tools both for technical decision-making and for optimizing communication. A reason why the PMO needs to exist will be their ability to continue to assess and implement AI tools that improve the project methodology, thereby providing increased value to the organization. The new PMO must rely less on existing software tools and embrace machine learning algorithms and other AI tools. The PMO can facilitate the ability for projects to take a holistic approach not only within a specific project but also across all projects in the program or portfolio. This is essential for project-based organizations. By providing a focus on data and making good decisions based on data, machine learning algorithms can actually reduce the complexity around projects.

The PMO must identify the most cost-effective projects and analyze the reasons and conditions that resulted in the cost-effective results. The objective is to replicate that set of conditions for the other projects. The PMO can push the capability of the organization and find ways to use the existing methodology for more challenging projects.

---

45 Press, "Cleaning Big Data."

Larger, geographically dispersed or more technologically complex projects can be completed because the methodology has now become a competitive advantage. The PMO can become an expert at managing an AI-infused process and offer expert consulting on how to achieve success.

To properly facilitate the new PMO, there must be a vigorous effort to manage project data, which will play a central role in successful results from AI tools. The PMO also needs to identify portfolio data, which may become useful for AI tools that work at a PMO level. For example, a dashboard of project metrics can be analyzed for both trends and possible negative project interactions. A new PMO dashboard must contain machine learning outcomes such as prediction of project success as well as schedule and cost projections based on historical data. The PMO needs to evaluate what machine learning algorithms are working the best and which ones must be revised or updated. Machine learning is unlike programs that are coded using a set of rules where there is either a correct answer or no answer at all. Machine learning builds a model that represents your project management data. In addition, the outcome of an algorithm might not produce a perfectly reliable result. In the face of having no other results, the PMO can develop guidelines on how the outcomes for such tools can be used. A result does not have to be perfect to be used for decision-making, but it must be properly understood. Perhaps the project needs to progress more and provide more data in order for the tool to be more accurate? Another consideration is to identify which machine learning algorithms are being used for prediction, for example. A neural network is commonly used, although there are times when other prediction methods, such as SVM, random forest, or Naive Bayes, are equally useful. Does your organization have some unique attribute that makes one type of algorithm inherently more successful than others? Obviously, this is an area where IT collaboration is important, although it makes more sense for the PMO to own this responsibility because they have a better overall organizational perspective.

With a new AI-based project methodology, the PMO becomes the caretaker of data and the learning process for the machine learning algorithms. They can produce new policies and procedures for each project manager to follow, but the PMO needs to monitor adherence, as any lapse in proper data management can degrade the value of a machine learning outcome. The new PMO will also have a role in managing stakeholders and communication. More specifically, there are concerns regarding the privacy of data and ethical considerations. Data is becoming more valuable due to machine learning tools because data is the nutrient that feeds the machine learning algorithms. Data security is critical for organizations that have sufficient historical project data to feed the AI tools, especially where the tools are producing consistently good results. To clearly understand the results being produced, the PMO staff needs more training in statistics because that is the basis for building machine learning models and using the results. AI tools can be invasive depending on how aggressive the organization wants to be when using all the capability of AI tools. Stakeholder habits and communication can be monitored and analyzed to build a psychological profile. This profile can then be used to more effectively manage the project stakeholder. What level of monitoring will be considered too much?

The PMO needs more input on how project managers are hired, the way that project managers are trained, and which project managers are assigned to specific projects. As the project methodology becomes enabled with AI tools, project manager training must move away from training for communication and leadership skills and toward managing data appropriately, understanding the mathematical results produced by AI tools, and how to interpret and best utilize AI results. Formal training in communication skills is a lesser priority because AI tools can be used to coach the project manager on how to optimize communication. AI tools can also be used to effectively motivate, persuade, and console stakeholders on an individual basis, depending on their personality profile and current emotional state. Project managers need a good grounding in math and statistics to understand how the data being fed to the machine learning algorithms is being used to identify correlations. Machine learning tools can effectively analyze data, but a human is required to add common sense into the results and to interpret the best way to move forward in the project. AI has difficulty with abstraction. As previously mentioned, an example of this is a robot that is trained to avoid walking into a wall, but it really has no idea what a wall is. The project manager uses higher-level understanding to implement machine learning results.

Based on these desired skills, the PMO will rethink how project managers are assigned to projects. Projects that require more effective communication with fragile stakeholders do not necessarily need to be assigned to a project manager who has the most training in interpersonal skills. This project can instead be assigned to a project manager who has demonstrated capability in implementing machine learning results and who uses personality profiles combined with AI suggestions to communicate to stakeholders. A smaller project where there is possibly less data to feed AI tools can be assigned to a project manager who is more skilled at managing on their own. To help AI tools be more effective with similar projects in the future, the project manager can then search for ways to gather more data from similar projects. The point of these examples is that the assignments for project managers will change and will no longer be based on normal or expected skills. The PMO must build an expertise in this new matrix of matching the best project managers or project teams to projects.

Project resources will also have new criteria for being allocated to a project. It might not be based on who is free or available at a given point in time. The new allocation is based on who is the best fit for each project when considering the entire portfolio of projects in the organization. Similarly, allocating funds for internal projects might be based on advancing the project methodology, the ability to implement a lean project that has the highest probability of success, and the project that is most aligned to the organization's goals.

The role of the PMO will expand to include much more interaction with other functional groups. The PMO in a project-based organization controls the knowledge that is needed to make the best decisions in other functional areas. For example, with an HR group, the PMO will recommend the new skill set required for project managers and project team members. When interacting with an IT group, the PMO will indicate the need for an effective data strategy and how to maintain and improve machine learning algorithms. For third-party vendors that are contracted through a procurement department, the PMO becomes a consultant to determine whether the vendors have and plan to deploy AI tools. The PMO determines whether the AI tools will be effective for the work required and whether the tools enhance the ability to deliver the full scope of the project on time and within budget. The PMO can require that vendors provide evidence of the effectiveness of their machine learning tools. They can ask about their AI methodology, hidden bias, and the data strategy that makes them a better choice than alternative vendors.

Another potential role for the PMO is to help develop the integrated IT approach with other tools in the digital transformation portfolio, such as IoT. The power of AI tools can be increased by combining it with other digital tools, but a sensible strategy needs to be developed. IoT is the technology of sensors that detect a change and can be used to automatically identify the status of various activities in a project. Using IoT also means a huge volume of additional data, especially streaming data, which will be available about the project and will need to be managed properly. Think of a self-driving car and all the sensors that communicate with each other. Can the PMO use a variety of digital tools to manage both projects and a portfolio more effectively? Perhaps IoT devices can be set up to communicate with other projects to track or optimize the dependencies. The PMO can determine where to place IoT sensors in order to provide valuable information on projects.

One of my research teams is working on using image recognition in construction projects to determine and provide regular feedback on the completion status. If the project work is performed outside, the project can aquire data from weather sensors or traffic data that can improve task efficiency because the project team is more prepared. Other digital transformation components include blockchain technology, big data, and quantum computing. The implementation of AI tools into the project process is a good learning process for the PMO. Based on that transition, a strategy can be developed for further technology that can improve project and portfolio efficiency.

COLLABORATING WITH IT RESOURCES

The IT department is undergoing significant changes. With an organization that has a focus on core competencies, databases are moving to the cloud and services are being outsourced. Third-party applications are widely used, as it does not make sense to create every software tool that is required. Another impending shift is with software applications themselves. If software is required to solve a problem, the old way was to code every branch of possibility, which results in a large program with many lines of code. The new method that is creeping into IT departments is to create a machine learning tool and let the data determine the result. The machine learning tool does not need to code every possible situation. Instead, it uses the data that applies to a specific situation, and this means many fewer lines of code to maintain. This all presupposes that PMO staff themselves are effectively trained in the use and implementation of AI tools. That training must include the importance of data and the ability to effectively interpret machine learning results. These are only some of the staffing considerations for the selection of the most effective project managers. The role of the PMO now takes on a new meaning with more authority in the organization because of their knowledge but also more responsibility to ensure that projects are delivered successfully.

Another possibility is to make ethical considerations a competitive advantage for the organization. Similar to the way some businesses market themselves as being environmentally responsible, the PMO can help promote the use of machine learning in an ethical way. In addition to policies and procedures that protect personal and data privacy, the AI tools themselves can be created in a more secure way. For example, the machine learning tool can learn and build a model from the data without retaining any of it. The organization can use personality profiles to improve communication but take steps to ensure that it is never considered as a work performance issue. The PMO can melt away a lot of personal bias by ensuring that work outcomes are the true measure of performance. As a project manager, I had employees covered in tattoos, dressed in unique clothing, and with streaks of different colors through their hair. Did it matter? The most important factor was whether they met performance expectations, and they usually met or exceeded them. You might be thinking that these employees should not be introduced to customers, but in some organizations, I found that the customers in that industry looked and dressed the same as my employees. The message is that AI tools are not judgmental, which is a positive characteristic.

An interesting comparison is how the PMO uses AI tools compared to a project manager. The PMO takes a higher-level perspective, for example, across several projects that all have a different probability of success and different levels of importance to the organization. The project manager uses AI tools to be more effective in completing projects. The PMO must ensure that project managers follow the new AI-based project methodology and are properly managing data. The PMO uses AI to manage project interdependencies, such as resources or dependent tasks. The PMO also needs to work with project managers to push the use of AI tools to another level of capability and to provide continuous improvement to the project processes. The PMO owns the project KPI metrics. In that responsibility, they track the success of both the projects being completed and the adherence to the policies and procedures defined in the new project methodology.

SUMMARY

Project management roles are changing, driven mainly by new technology and environmental factors. It is important for the PMO to understand the implications of change and to manage it properly. In the near term, project managers must be collaborators with AI tools, and this role requires a good understanding of statistics, the ability to interpret machine learning results, and a positive attitude that embraces change. These factors will become the new criteria for being a successful project manager as AI tools are deployed. AI capability is likely to play a larger role in communication. Project managers learn how to communicate with virtual team members, which may shift to include a team consisting of some humans and some AI-based team members. The PMO needs to make all this successful and demonstrate to the organization the value of implementing AI tools in the project methodology. The deployment of AI tools by the PMO happens while projects are still being executed and the organization is undergoing other changes. This is not an easy task. The PMO is responsible for both the change in project methodology and the speed of project management change that can be successfully absorbed by the organization.

CHAPTER 11

The Future of AI and the PMO

This profession deserves a better project methodology, and we are the ones who can make it happen.

Technological advancement is relentless, and AI functionality continues to grow exponentially as research funding increases. Projects are becoming more complex and the status quo is no longer optional. Organizations struggle to find the best project implementation strategy, and now AI has the solution to at least some of the problems. We are at the beginning of a revolution in project methods, and all project managers must adapt to these new ways to successfully manage projects.

Executive leaders are being inundated with the message that they must embrace and implement digital transformation to survive as an organization. This includes changing products, services, and processes in order to adopt advanced technology, such as data mining, AI, and IoT. The paradox is that as they embark on this transformation, the project methodology used to deliver the change will not contain or utilize any of that advanced technology. Isn't this a bizarre situation? In a normal world, the project methodology would be changed first and then used to successfully implement the advanced technology into organizations. The obvious question is going to be whether or not the implementation fails because the concept of deploying the technology was flawed or the project methodology was inadequate. This needs to be addressed by the PMO and, in fact, all project leaders. The survival of organizations depends on projects successfully delivering change, and the project processes must be radically altered to deliver the results.

TRENDS AND CHALLENGES

Digital transformation is the term for a strategy to improve organizational results by incorporating new technology. From numerous surveys, executives of organizations appear eager to take advantage of new technology, but the obstacle appears to be middle managers who are not sure how to proceed.[46] There must be a defined strategy for new technology, and AI will be part of that strategy. The components may include any of the following: data mining, IoT, blockchain, quantum computing, and, of course, AI. The good news for the PMO is that funding should be available, although the funding may not appear without a solid business case and, of course, an information technology strategy. Project management changes are simply about changing the processes around making better decisions based on data. Tools such as IoT, blockchain, and quantum computing can be incorporated into the strategy, but AI is the main component. The PMO needs to find a way to convince executives that using AI to change project processes is necessary and fits nicely in any technology roadmap. Data mining is probably the best first step to justify the implementation of machine learning algorithms. Of course, there will be synergies with other technologies, but the maturity and practicality of each technology is different. AI has capabilities that can be implemented now and modified as the roadmap evolves.

Academic research is already being performed on the next concept to take language comprehension by machines to another level. The research is called grounded language and picks up on Alan Turing's suggestion that a simple machine learning algorithm can be built and then trained to continuously learn.[47] This research combines cognitive and developmental psychology and uses reinforcement learning that includes verbal instructions and visual information. It is similar to the example of a child who continues to learn over time. Grounded language is the process of trying to emulate this process using a curriculum

---

46 Shapiro, "AI Gap Analysis."
47 Maxime Chevalier-Boisvert, Dzmitry Bahdanau, Salem Lahlou, Lucas Willems, Chitwan Saharia, Thien Huu Nguyen, and Yoshua Bengio, "BabyAI: A Platform to Study the Sample Efficiency of Grounded Language Learning" (presentation, ICLR Conference, New Orleans, LA, May 6–9, 2019).

approach to teach basic language and then train more complicated concepts later. This is different in that researchers are trying to develop a machine that understands the meaning of a word such as *red*. Current NLP technology does not know the meaning of words because it uses statistics to treat them as data to arrive at what appears to be language understanding. Words have meaning. In the future, interactions with an AI tool will be similar to a human project manager, except that we will expect more rational and correct decisions from the nonhuman.

Research continues with a concept known as deep learning. This is the ability for an AI tool to perform reasoning instead of simply evaluating data. A lot of human knowledge is amassed over time and is not readily available to AI. If a project team member is not feeling well, they might not perform to their normal standard, something an AI tool has difficulty making a correlation to. As mentioned previously, an AI tool can detect a wall but does not realize that if the wall is simply a piece of fabric draped over a bar, it can proceed through the fabric. Humans understand that if you leave loose garbage at the end of your driveway on a windy day, it might blow into your neighbor's yard. A robot might have difficulty interpreting this reasoning, and this is the next challenge for AI. It includes the ability to learn common sense and to understand that unexpected changes happen and can have unanticipated consequences. An AI tool that achieves this level of development will be truly disruptive in project management.

One of the possible methods for deep learning to be successful is unsupervised learning where there are no labeled datasets. With supervised learning, it takes many iterations to "teach" the model with the given data. This is not the same in unsupervised learning. A child does not need to see five hundred images of a cat before recognizing a new image as a cat. What does this mean for project management? Being a new project manager is somewhat like being a child. We may have project management training, but it is the practice and experience of delivering projects that makes us good project managers. Obviously, more experienced project managers have an advantage over new project managers. However, older project managers still make errors and bad decisions that may not be exhibited by new project managers who know how to use AI tools. Humans have the ability to foresee the possible results of decisions. This can be exciting for us, for example, when we see a performer attempting a precarious feat such as walking across a tightrope. We foresee a probability that they might fail. Similarly, in a project, a lot of project managers get a feeling when something bad is about to happen. We call it intuition, although it is really an interpretation of our knowledge and how our experiences provide insight into the probability of what might go wrong. For a machine learning algorithm, a similar process is to use historical data to forecast project issues that have not happened yet but that have a high probability of occurring. Can we use unsupervised learning to evaluate the current situation and current status and then forecast a negative event?

Even greater is the ability to combine a form of unsupervised learning with reinforcement learning. We see this now in robots as simple as the Roomba that vacuums a floor and uses sensors to detect obstacles. Some robots learn the pattern of the room by mapping the obstacles or bumping into them. It would be amazing if we could learn from every mistake in every event that happened in a project and then guide a new project to an easily successful conclusion. The processes are in the early stage of development but are powerful possibilities that can be applied directly to projects.

ETHICS AND PRIVACY

As AI tools are introduced into project management processes, the PMO will have some responsibility for the security of the data as well as for protecting personal privacy rights based on how the data is used. AI tools will become more integrated into everything we do as humans, so there is increasing concern regarding data security and privacy of our personal information. The problem is that the technology is so new that it is difficult to know what approach will work the best. Researchers and technology implementors are encouraged to join the FATE (Fairness, Accountability, Transparency, and Ethics) movement to provide some level of responsibility for developing and using AI in a way that is not harmful to humans. This is an approach supported by Microsoft. Google initiated a different approach by creating an external AI ethics board to oversee responsible development of AI at Google. After one week, the board was dissolved due to employees' concerns over the integrity of the board members.[48] The European Union published ethical guidelines for trustworthy AI that say that AI development should result in a product that is lawful, ethical, and robust. The term *robust* is interpreted to mean that it should function properly when deployed but should also meet the ethical and lawful criteria as time passes and as more data is added, especially from the social environment. The guidelines include seven more clearly defined requirements.[49] While these movements are encouraging, they are only indicators that global agreement on ethical AI development will be extremely difficult, if not impossible.

Ethics is a large concern that covers many areas. One problem is with extremely biased AI tools that, based on data, perform unintended profiling of individuals. In other words, there is a bias in historical data toward stereotypes. This might include women not becoming corporate executives or minorities being more prone to crime. Historical data sucks. As humans, most of us understand the need to progress and to become inclusive because that is really what makes us human—the ability to be kind, forgiving, and welcoming. AI tools that

---

[48] Kelsey Piper, "Google Cancels AI Ethics Board in Response to Outcry," Vox, April 4, 2019, http://www.vox.com/future-perfect/2019/4/4/18295933/google-cancels-ai-ethics-board.

[49] European Commission, "Ethics Guidelines for Trustworthy AI," April 8, 2019, https://ec.europa.eu/digital-single-market/en/news/ethics-guidelines-trustworthy-ai.

use historical data have the ability to include prejudicial judgments and to use them in decision-making. We must identify and eliminate that hidden bias in machine learning algorithms in order to move forward in a professional and human way. The initiatives so far are scattered and there is no standard to incorporate into the organization's policies, so for now PMOs need to be aware and implement their own standards to ensure that AI is used ethically. This will be a large and thankless responsibility, although at some point in the future, the value of this responsibility will become clear when an organization manages to avoid a massive ethical mistake that becomes public with similar massive negative consequences.

Another ethical issue that the PMO will likely face is how AI tools assess employee performance. Current tools analyze how efficient team members are at completing a task and then may recommend a replacement based on habitually slower work. Is that fair? What is affecting the individual's work habit? Is this week an aberration in their normal energy level? What is the level of inefficiency where an analytics tool determines that the individual needs to be replaced, and how is that calculated? Allowing AI tools to use project data is expected, but decisions must be considered carefully when the data is related to the individuals on the project. There must be a policy on how much of their digital footprint is retained and used. For project efficiency, data needs to be collected on the length of time it takes a person to complete a task, unless this information is used in a negative way, such as removing the team member for poor performance. There is a proper process to manage performance issues, and it should not involve data that is originally being collected for AI tools and then diverted for another purpose.

Another controversial area will be the collection of verbal and written communication to build a personality profile or to identify personal psychological traits. This is currently gathered for marketing purposes with our internet clicks. It can be collected in a project environment, but the danger is if it is used for manipulative purposes or even provided without permission to a third party. In all cases, the use of personal data from a project must be communicated clearly and in advance to those involved. While the organization is responsible for these policies and decisions, it is likely that a PMO will be caught in the middle as more AI tools are implemented. The PMO must adhere to organizational rules but also must protect and motivate valuable project team members. Data privacy is always an ongoing concern, and the PMO needs to find a way to guarantee that personal information is not used in an unprofessional manner. Yes, we give up much of our privacy by creating a Facebook page, using a points card when shopping, and freely giving away personal information because we want to win that local raffle. It is different in an organization and in a project. In that situation, people are reliant on the organization to protect their privacy and not mishandle or lose it in a grand misadventure or breach of security. While this is clearly an organizational issue, the implications have an impact on a project level. Project team members need more than a feeling of being valued by the organization; they also need to feel protected while they work on organizational tasks.

Security is a concern with data because it represents the essence of the organization. For organizations that receive and utilize user data, there is an obligation to ensure that it is secure and not leaked to or breached by any unauthorized group. When using machine learning tools, the algorithm and outcome are important but the data is essential, as any organization that has access to the data will be able to replicate the results. A competing organization can benefit from acquiring additional data to improve their own AI results. The data does not have to be "stolen" to build a successful model because the algorithm needs only to read the data to create a model. This adds a new level of concern for data. Will an intruder be able to access the data, read it, then leave it as if no intrusion ever occurred? Detecting data breaches will become more difficult, so this makes it even more important to protect an organization's data.

SUMMARY

As with any new technology, there will be issues to face and unpleasant consequences for ignoring them. For implementation of AI tools in project management, two overriding issues will be ethical concerns and data privacy, and both of these will have an impact on the PMO unless they are addressed properly. Ethical concerns in how AI is used will have an effect on all stakeholders, especially the project team, and it is never a good plan to disillusion the people who are trying to complete the work. In addition to policies around how personal data is captured, analyzed, and used, the content must be well protected from leaking to unauthorized individuals. In case it is not obvious by now, an organization's project data is a critical component for increasing productivity and improving the bottom line. As time progresses, a variety of new attacks can be expected on data, and the organization must find ways to secure this valuable asset.

CHAPTER 12
Conclusion

We tend to overestimate the effect of a technology in the short run and underestimate it in the long run.[50]
—Amara's law

---

50 Susan Ratcliffe, ed., *Oxford Essential Quotations*, 4th ed. (New York: Oxford University Press, 2016).

Near the beginning of the book, I described several ways for the PMO to be instrumental in improving the bottom line for their organization through improved project management processes. The first suggestion is to use AI to develop a more accurate scope statement, schedule, and budget. This is more than a suggestion—I implore you to do this to increase project success rates, and subsequently, the credibility for the new methodology. Use the predicator tools to gauge the probability of success and, where required, review and update the planning documents. The concept is simply to get the project off to a great start instead of a maybe or not-so-great start.

The next activity for the PMO is to find ways to reduce the project implementation cost. This not only benefits an internal organization but also can be a huge competitive advantage when performing projects as a vendor. This assumes that the lower bid still includes the ability to complete the project successfully. Imagine the results if competitors lower their bids and are unable to complete the project successfully, probably overspending to what should have been their original bid. This is where the advantage of a new process that uses AI tools is obvious and compelling for customers. The path to lower costs requires increased efficiency in all the executing aspects of the project. This includes resourcing, communicating, and managing every day-to-day issue in a way that provides an optimized solution. Lean processes can be used within an AI-infused project management methodology to eliminate waste and improve the bottom line. Data mining and machine learning capability are critical elements for these improvements. An obvious cost reduction is the ability to make project managers more efficient and possibly reduce the amount of time required for each project. In spite of the content that outlines how to reduce or eliminate the project manager, it is not something I advocate, especially at the start of AI implementation. However, the project managers who are assigned to projects must be trained in AI interpretation and be willing to collaborate with AI tools.

Success can be inspiring, and as an organization develops a robust new project methodology, there is an opportunity to use that methodology to expand project capacity and capability. The PMO must lead this effort. Embrace the change and be confident in the proficiency of a successful project process based on new technology. Depending on the willingness of the organization's culture toward risk, the PMO can help determine the rate of change. This is one example of how the PMO can successfully implement change and promote top-line growth for the organization.

Project management as a profession is at a pivotal moment in history, and the PMO has a crucial role to play in changing how we manage projects. The status quo is not acceptable, given the low project success rates and increasing complexity of managing projects. The PMO can be at the forefront of developing a new project methodology by incorporating AI technology or be relegated to an afterthought as time marches on. The PMO has an opportunity to lead their organization into a thoughtful, well-executed, and value-driven change to project management that will result in a competitive, highly respected, and successful organization. The alternative is a messy and harsh reality. Improving the bottom line requires increased efficiencies, and the PMO is fully capable of finding incredible improvements in the way that we manage projects. It is my hope that this book helps that journey.

Acknowledgments

Somehow this second book followed naturally from the first one. I had much more to write and decided to focus the content at a higher level, the PMO. As I continue to learn and embrace the AI experience with my colleagues, clients, and connections, I plan to share my knowledge. This is a fast-paced technology, and we all need to participate in developing our skills or we may get left behind. I am excited by the opportunity that AI offers to project management, and I offer a big thanks to everyone who has encouraged and supported my efforts in this field.

Thanks once again to the amazing people I work with in the project management program at Algonquin College in Ottawa, Canada. Special thanks to Angela and Nicole. Huge thanks to Lathif, who kept prompting me with new ideas and concepts. Thanks to my beta readers once again, Lorraine and Kelly, who are both amazing project managers. Thanks to my wife, Jill, who never waivers in her support.

Thanks to the work from my volunteer research team, Anuj, Rohan P., and Jit. Thanks to Kevin and Spencer, (and Anuj again) for leading the software team in taking the predictor tool development to a new level. Thank you to my graphic artist, Mila, who produced the images in both books, and to my main reviewer, Caitlin, for her insightful feedback. Thanks to David Barrett for helping me be a better speaker, especially in how to answer questions from the audience, and for producing a great podcast. Thank you to the local PMI chapter and to all my students and attendees who come to listen to me speak, cheer, applaud, and ask interesting questions.

My classroom is like a second home. It is place where we all learn more about project management and, at the same time, have a bit of fun.

Abbreviations

AI	artificial intelligence
CRM	customer relationship management
ERP	enterprise resource planning
EVM	earned value management
HR	human resources
IoT	Internet of Things
IT	information technology
KPI	key performance indicator
NLP	natural language processing
PMBOK	Project Management Body of Knowledge
PMI	Project Management Institute
PMO	project management office
RFP	request for proposal
ROI	return on investment

SV	schedule variance
SVM	support vector machine
TOC	theory of constraints
VAC	variance at completion
WBS	work breakdown structure

Bibliography

Armitage, Hanae. "AI Matched, Outperformed Radiologists in Screening X-Rays for Certain Diseases." Medical Xpress. November 21, 2018. https://medicalxpress.com/news/2018-11-ai-outperformed-radiologists-screening-x-rays.html.

Bertallee, Celina. "New Study: 64% of People Trust a Robot More Than Their Manager." Oracle. October 15, 2019. https://www.oracle.com/corporate/pressrelease/robots-at-work-101519.html.

Bostrom, Nick. *Superintelligence: Paths, Dangers, Strategies*. New York: Oxford University Press, 2016.

Boudreau, Paul. *Applying Artificial Intelligence to Project Management*. New York: Elite Authors, 2019.

Cavallo, Jo. "Confronting the Criticisms Facing Watson for Oncology." *ASCO Post*. September 10, 2019. https://ascopost.com/issues/september-10-2019/confronting-the-criticisms-facing-watson-for-oncology.

Chevalier-Boisvert, Maxime, Dzmitry Bahdanau, Salem Lahlou, Lucas Willems, Chitwan Saharia, Thien Huu Nguyen, and Yoshua Bengio.

"BabyAI: A Platform to Study the Sample Efficiency of Grounded Language Learning." Presentation at the ICLR Conference, New Orleans, LA, May 6–9, 2019.

Davenport, Thomas H. *The AI Advantage: How to Put the Artificial Intelligence Revolution to Work.* Cambridge, MA: MIT Press, 2018.

Dietrich, Perttu, Karlos A. Artto, and Jaakko Kujala. "Strategic Priorities and PMO Functions in Project-Based Firms." Paper presented at the PMI Research Conference: Defining the Future of Project Management, Washington, DC, July 14, 2010.

Domingos, Pedro. *The Master Algorithm: How the Quest for the Ultimate Learning Machine Will Remake Our World.* New York: Basic Books, 2018.

European Commission. "Ethics Guidelines for Trustworthy AI." April 8, 2019. https://ec.europa.eu/digital-single-market/en/news/ethics-guidelines-trustworthy-ai.

Forbes Technology Council. "13 Industries Soon to Be Revolutionized by Artificial Intelligence." *Forbes.* January 16, 2019. https://www.forbes.com/sites/forbestechcouncil/2019/01/16/13-industries-soon-to-be-revolutionized-by-artificial-intelligence/#6da2a753dc18.

Ford, Martin. *Architects of Intelligence: The Truth about AI from the People Building It.* Birmingham, UK: Packt, 2018.

Friedman, Ellen. "With Machine Learning and AI, the Win Isn't Always Where You Think." Mapr. April 30, 2019. https://mapr.com/blog/

with-machine-learning-and-ai-the-win-isnt-always-where-you-think.

Goldratt, Eli. *Critical Chain: Project Management and the Theory of Constraints.* Prince Frederick, MD: HighBridge, 2014. Audiobook.

Gomes, Leonardo Augusto de Vasconcelos, Vinicius Chagas Brasil, Rafael Augusto Seixas Reis de Paula, Ana Lúcia Figueiredo Facin, Frederico César de Vasconcelos Gomes, and Mario Sergio Salerno. "Proposing a Multilevel Approach for the Management of Uncertainties in Exploratory Projects." *PMI Journal* 50, no. 5 (2019): 554–70.

Google Duplex. "A.I. Assistant Calls Local Businesses to Make Appointments." YouTube. May 8, 2018. https://www.youtube.com/watch?v=D5VN56jQMWM.

Guszcza, James, Iyad Rahwan, Will Bible, Manuel Cebrian, and Vic Katyal. "Why We Need to Audit Algorithms." *Harvard Business Review.* November 28, 2018. https://hbr.org/2018/11/why-we-need-to-audit-algorithms.

Horaczek, Stan. "The Role of Humans in Self-Driving Cars Is Even More Complicated after Uber's Fatal Crash." *Popular Science.* March 23, 2018. https://www.popsci.com/human-drivers-and-self-driving-car.

Hutson, Matthew. "How Artificial Intelligence Could Negotiate Better Deals for Humans." *Science Magazine.* September 11, 2017. https://www.sciencemag.org/news/2017/09/how-artificial-intelligence-could-negotiate-better-deals-humans.

Jones, Capers, and Olivier Bonsignour. *The Economics of Software Quality*. Boston: Addison-Wesley Professional, 2011.

Kelnar, Dan. "The State of AI: Divergence 2019." MMC Ventures Report. 2019. https://www.mmcventures.com/wp-content/uploads/2019/02/The-State-of-AI-2019-Divergence.pdf.

Kock, Alexander, and Hans Georg Gemünden. "Project Lineage Management and Project Portfolio Success." *PMI Journal* 50, no. 5 (2019): 587–601.

Kruse, Kevin. "30% of Workers Would Replace Their Boss with a Robot." *Forbes*. September 18, 2019. https://www.forbes.com/sites/kevinkruse/2019/09/18/30-of-workers-would-replace-their-boss-with-a-robot/#28c4ed017eeb.

Lahmann, Marc. "Would You Trust a Machine to Run Your Project Portfolio?" *PwC Magazine*. Accessed November 15, 2019. https://www.pwc.ch/en/insights/disclose/30/transformation-assurance-would-you-trust-a-machine-to-run-your-project-portfolio.html.

Levy, Heather Pemberton. "Gartner Predicts a World of Exponential Change." Smarter with Gartner. October 18, 2016. https://www.gartner.com/smarterwithgartner/gartner-predicts-a-virtual-world-of-exponential-change.

Ortega, Mary. "PMI 2017 Pulse of the Profession: Project Success Rates Climb, Fewer Dollars Wasted." Project Management Institute. February 8, 2017. https://www.pmi.org/about/press-media/press-releases/pmi-2017-pulse-of-the-profession.

Piper, Kelsey. "Google Cancels AI Ethics Board in Response to Outcry." Vox. April 4, 2019. https://www.vox.com/future-perfect/2019/4/4/18295933/google-cancels-ai-ethics-board.

Press, Gil. "Cleaning Big Data: Most Time-Consuming, Least Enjoyable Data Science Task, Survey Says." *Forbes*. March 23, 2016. https://www.forbes.com/sites/gilpress/2016/03/23/data-preparation-most-time-consuming-least-enjoyable-data-science-task-survey-says/#11ec00896f63.

Project Management Institute. *A Guide to the Project Management Body of Knowledge* (PMBOK Guide). 6th ed. Newton Square, PA: Project Management Institute, 2017.

Ratcliffe, Susan, ed. *Oxford Essential Quotations*. 4th ed. New York: Oxford University Press, 2016.

Ray, Sunil. "Commonly Used Machine Learning Algorithms (with Python and R Codes)." Analytics Vidhya. September 9, 2017. https://www.analyticsvidhya.com/blog/2017/09/common-machine-learning-algorithms.

Receptiviti.com. "Understand the People Who Matter to Your Business." Accessed January 9, 2020. https://www.receptiviti.com.

Rieger, Sarah. "At Least Two Malls Are Using Facial Recognition Technology to Track Shoppers' Ages and Genders without Telling." CBC News. July 27, 2018. https://www.cbc.ca/news/canada/calgary/calgary-malls-1.4760964.

Rochefort, Steve. "Practical Challenges in ML Workflows." Lecture presented at Machine Learning and Artificial Intelligence Ottawa, Ontario, CA, September 9, 2019.

Roseke, Bernie. "10 Roles and Responsibilities of a PMO." ProjectEngineer. February 15, 2019. https://www.projectengineer.net/10-roles-and-responsibilities-of-a-pmo.

RT News. "Is a Bicycle Alive? Can an Elephant Fit through a House Door? DARPA to Teach AI 'Common Sense.'" October 14, 2018. https://www.rt.com/news/441237-darpa-ai-common-sense.

Rumeser, David, and Margaret Emsley. "Can Serious Games Improve Project Management Decision Making under Complexity?" *PMI Journal* 50, no. 5 (2019): 23–39.

Sahota, Neil, and Michael Ashley. *Own the A.I. Revolution: Unlock Your Artificial Intelligence Strategy to Disrupt Your Competition*. New York: McGraw-Hill Education, 2019.

Schneider, Christie. "The Biggest Data Challenges That You Might Not Even Know You Have." IBM. May 25, 2016. https://www.ibm.com/blogs/watson/2016/05/biggest-data-challenges-might-not-even-know.

Seibel, Thomas. *Digital Transformation: Survive and Thrive in an Era of Mass Extinction*. New York: Rosetta Books, 2019.

Shapiro, Daniel. "AI Gap Analysis." Lecture presented at Machine Learning and Artificial Intelligence Ottawa, Ontario, CA, October, 28, 2019.

Shapiro, Daniel, and Khalid El Emam. "Managing the Risks from AI Algorithms." Replica Analytics. December 10, 2019. https://replica-analytics.com/blog/blog/risks-from-AI-algorithms.

Silver, David, Thomas Hubert, Julian Schrittwieser, and Demis Hassabis. "AlphaZero: Shedding New Light on Chess, Shogi, and Go." DeepMind. December 6, 2018. https://deepmind.com/blog/article/alphazero-shedding-new-light-grand-games-chess-shogi-and-go.

SmartBear.com. "Artificial Intelligence for Faster and Smarter UI Testing." Accessed November 26, 2019. https://smartbear.com/resources/ebooks/artificial-intelligence-for-faster-and-smarter-ui.

Smith, John R. "IBM Research Takes Watson to Hollywood with the First 'Cognitive Movie Trailer.'" IBM. August 31, 2016. https://www.ibm.com/blogs/think/2016/08/cognitive-movie-trailer.

Snorkel.org. "Programmatically Building and Managing Training Data." Accessed January 9, 2020. https://www.snorkel.org.

Strickland, Eliza. "How IBM Watson Overpromised and Underdelivered on AI Health Care." IEEE Spectrum. April 2, 2019. https://spectrum.ieee.org/biomedical/diagnostics/how-ibm-watson-overpromised-and-underdelivered-on-ai-health-care.

Subramanian, Sandeep, Raymond Li, Jonathan Pilault, and Christopher Pal. "On Extractive and Abstractive Neural Document Summarization with Transformer Language Models." Cornell University. September 7, 2019. https://arxiv.org/abs/1909.03186.

Trifacta.com. "What Is Data Wrangling?" Accessed January 9, 2020. https://www.trifacta.com/data-wrangling.

Vanian, Jonathan. "Most Executives Fear Their Companies Will Fail if They Don't Adopt A.I." *Fortune*. November 14, 2019. https://fortune.com/2019/11/14/executives-fear-accenture-a-i.

Yao, Mariya. "6 Ways AI Transforms How We Develop Software." *Forbes*. April 18, 2018. https://www.forbes.com/sites/mariyayao/2018/04/18/6-ways-ai-transforms-how-we-develop-software/#7490122c26cf.

Zijderveld, Gabi. "Our Evolution from Emotion AI to Human Perception AI." Affectiva. April 2, 2019. https://blog.affectiva.com/our-evolution-from-emotion-ai-to-human-perception-ai.

About the Author

Paul Boudreau, PMP, is a highly respected and influential project management professional with more than thirty-five years in the technology industry. His extensive project management experience includes successful project implementations in Canada, the United States, and the United Kingdom. He uses his in-depth knowledge of project management to research and develop AI concepts, following his passion to improve project success rates. Paul's first book, *Applying Artificial Intelligence to Project Management*, was well received for both professional and practical insights into a complex new technology. As a college professor and public speaker at project management events, Paul is dynamic and motivational as he presents visual images and compelling arguments for using AI to change the project methodology.

Paul lives in Ottawa, where he pursues his lifelong ambition to teach, write, and inspire young project managers. He enjoys relaxing at his cottage with his wife, Jill, and their two dogs.

www.ingramcontent.com/pod-product-compliance
Lightning Source LLC
Chambersburg PA
CBHW060833220526
45466CB00003B/1089